access t[o]

The **INTERREGNUM**

Second Edition

Michael Lynch

Hodder & Stoughton

A MEMBER OF THE HODDER HEADLINE GROUP

Acknowledgements

The cover illustration is a miniature portrait of Oliver Cromwell by Samuel Cooper (courtesy of the Bridgeman private collection).

The Publishers would like to thank the following for permission to reproduce material in this volume:

J.P. Kenyon, *The Stuart Constitution, 1603–1688, Documents and Commentary*, 2nd edition, 1986 reproduced by kind permission of Cambridge University Press; *Speeches of Oliver Cromwell* edited by Ivan Roots and published by J.M. Dent reproduced by kind permission of J.M. Dent; Barry Coward, *Oliver Cromwell*, Longman 1991 copyright Longman Group UK Ltd 1991; Derek Hirst, *Authority and Conflict: England 1603–1658*, Edward Arnold 1986, reprinted by kind permission of Hodder Arnold.

The publishers would like to thank the following for permission to reproduce copyright illustrations in this volume:

The Fotomas Index, pages 11, 23, 57, 62, 93, 115; The British Library, page 24; and The Cromwell Museum, page 61.

Every effort has been made to trace and acknowledge ownership of copyright. The Publishers will be glad to make suitable arrangements with any copyright holders whom it has not been possible to contact.

Orders: please contact Bookpoint Ltd, 130 Milton Park, Abingdon, Oxon OX14 4SB. Telephone (44) 01235 827720, Fax: (44) 01235 400454. Lines are open from 9.00–6.00, Monday to Saturday, with a 24-hour message answering service. Email address: orders@bookpoint.co.uk

British Library Cataloguing in Publication Data
A catalogue record for this title is available from the British Library

ISBN 0 340 84580 5

First published 2002
Impression number   10 9 8 7 6 5 4 3 2 1
Year   2007 2006 2005 2004 2003 2002

Copyright © 2002 Michael Lynch

Typeset by Fakenham Photosetting Limited, Fakenham, Norfolk
Printed in Great Britain for Hodder & Stoughton Educational, a division of Hodder Headline Plc, 338 Euston Road, London NW1 3BH by Bath Press Ltd, England.

Contents

Preface

To the general reader

Although the *Access to History* series has been designed with the needs of students studying the subject at higher examination levels very much in mind, it also has a great deal to offer the general reader. The main body of the text (i.e. ignoring the 'Study Guides' at the ends of chapters) forms a readable and yet stimulating survey of a coherent topic as studied by historians. However, each author's aim has not merely been to provide a clear explanation of what happened in the past (to interest and inform): it has also been assumed that most readers wish to be stimulated into thinking further about the topic and to form opinions of their own about the significance of the events that are described and discussed (to be challenged). Thus, although no prior knowledge of the topic is expected on the reader's part, she or he is treated as an intelligent and thinking person throughout. The author tends to share ideas and possibilities with the reader, rather than passing on numbers of so-called 'historical truths'.

To the student reader

Although advantage has been taken of the publication of a second edition to ensure the results of recent research are reflected in the text, the main alteration from the first edition is the inclusion of new features, and the modification of existing ones, aimed at assisting you in your study of the topic at AS level, A level and Higher. Two features are designed to assist you during your first reading of a chapter. The *Points to Consider* section following each chapter title is intended to focus your attention on the main theme(s) of the chapter, and the issues box following most section headings alerts you to the question or questions to be dealt with in the section. The *Working on ...* section at the end of each chapter suggests ways of gaining maximum benefit from the chapter.

There are many ways in which the series can be used by students studying History at a higher level. It will, therefore, be worthwhile thinking about your own study strategy before you start your work on this book. Obviously, your strategy will vary depending on the aim you have in mind, and the time for study that is available to you.

If, for example, you want to acquire a general overview of the topic in the shortest possible time, the following approach will probably be the most effective:

1. Read chapter 1. As you do so, keep in mind the issues raised in the *Points to Consider* section.
2. Read the *Points to Consider* section at the beginning of chapter 2 and decide whether it is necessary for you to read this chapter.
3. If it is, read the chapter, stopping at each heading or sub-heading to note

down the main points that have been made. Often, the best way of doing this is to answer the question(s) posed in the Key Issues boxes.
4. Repeat stage 2 (and stage 3 where appropriate) for all the other chapters.

If, however, your aim is to gain a thorough grasp of the topic, taking however much time is necessary to do so, you may benefit from carrying out the same procedure with each chapter, as follows:

1. Try to read the chapter in one sitting. As you do this, bear in mind any advice given in the *Points to Consider* section.
2. Study the flow diagram at the end of the chapter, ensuring that you understand the general 'shape' of what you have just read.
3. Read the *Working on...* section and decide what further work you need to do on the chapter. In particularly important sections of the book, this is likely to involve reading the chapter a second time and stopping at each heading and sub-heading to think about (and probably to write a summary of) what you have just read.
4. Attempt the *Source-based questions* section. It will sometimes be sufficient to think through your answers, but additional understanding will often be gained by forcing yourself to write them down.

When you have finished the main chapters of the book, study the 'Further Reading' section and decide what additional reading (if any) you will do on the topic.

This book has been designed to help make your studies both enjoyable and successful. If you can think of ways in which this could have been done more effectively, please contact us. In the meantime, we hope that you will gain greatly from your study of History.

Keith Randell & Robert Pearce

Introduction

POINTS TO CONSIDER

The Interregnum covered the years between the execution of Charles I in 1649, on the orders of Parliament, and the restoration of his son, Charles II, in 1660, at the invitation of Parliament. Your first aim in reading this chapter is to understand why such an extraordinary cycle of events occurred. To do this successfully, you need to grasp the main details and character of the events of the years which preceded the Interregnum. That is why the chapter begins with a survey of the major developments of the reign of Charles I, 1625–49. If you acquaint yourself with this survey, you will then be in a good position to understand the key features of the Interregnum itself, which is surveyed in the second section of the chapter. When you have studied these sections, you should then turn to the final part of the chapter, which introduces you to some of the major historical interpretations of the Interregnum.

KEY DATES

1625		Accession of Charles I.
1625–29		Charles experienced difficulties with his parliaments.
1629–40		The period of non-parliamentary government.
1637–40		The Bishops' Wars.
1640	April	Parliament recalled, but dissolved after 4 weeks.
	Nov	Parliament recalled.
1641	May	Strafford executed.
	Oct	Rebellion in Ireland.
		The Grand Remonstrance presented.
		The 'Root and Branch Petition' presented.
1642	Jan	Charles failed to arrest the 5 members.
	Mar	Parliament issued militia ordinance.
	June	Charles rejected Parliament's 19 Propositions.
	Aug	Outbreak of civil war.
1643	Sept	Parliament signed Solemn League and Covenant with the Scots.
1644		Battle of Marston Moor.
1645		Formation of New Model Army under Cromwell.
1646	May	Charles surrendered to the Scots.
1646–48		Charles attempted to play off the Scots, Parliament and the army against each other.
1647		Charles signed an 'Engagement' with the Scots.
1648	April	Second civil war started.
	Aug	War ended with Charles's defeat.
	Dec	Pride's Purge prepared the way for the King's trial and execution.

1 Outline of the Period, 1625–49

a) Problems in the Early Years of Charles I's reign, 1625–40

> **KEY ISSUE** Why did Charles attempt to govern without Parliament between 1629 and 1640?

Charles, who came to the throne in 1625, had been angered during the earlier years of his reign by Parliament's criticism of his foreign, religious and financial policies. After 1629 he deliberately avoided summoning Parliament. During the following 11 years his royal government tried to develop a method of revenue-raising that would end its reliance on parliamentary finance. The royal power was invoked to impose heavy taxation and high customs levies. This proved a deeply unpopular policy with the landowning and merchant classes. The most notorious measure was the raising of ship money, a use of the ancient right of the monarch to levy taxes from the maritime counties for the maintenance of the navy in wartime. Ship money became particularly resented since it was now levied in peacetime and was extended to include the inland counties.

Matters were complicated by the issue of religion. Since the Reformation a century earlier, which had involved the rejection of Papal authority in England, the Anglican (English) Church had developed as a broadly Protestant body. By Charles I's time, two main strands were identifiable within it, Puritanism and Arminianism. Puritanism had no exact definition. It referred broadly to those Protestants who detested Popery (Roman Catholicism) and were resentful of episcopacy, the church system that gave power to bishops and priests and that demanded uniformity of worship. Puritans also frowned upon the trappings of religious worship. They disliked elaborate ritual and ceremony, believing that these hindered direct communication between God and his people. It is important to remember that, up to the period of conflict with which this book deals, Puritanism was not a separate denomination; it was contained within the Anglican Church.

Arminianism, which was the major influence among the bishops and higher clergy of the Church, laid emphasis upon hierarchy, the notion of ascending layers of authority within the Church: obedience was owed by the laity to the parish clergy, by the clergy to the bishops, by the bishops to the archbishops. It stressed the importance of the sacraments and the ritual of worship. Arminianism became the policy of the Church under William Laud, who was appointed Archbishop of Canterbury in 1633. Laud was a devoted servant of the Crown who believed it was his duty to impose religious conformity and obedience. The zeal with which he pursued this aim was one of the main causes of the royal government's unpopularity during this period of the so-called 'eleven-year tyranny'. Using the Church courts and the prerogative courts (those which stood outside the common law of the realm and depended on the king's authority for their power), Laud harried those who would not conform. The imposition of the Prayer Book, which laid down detailed regulations about the way in which public worship in the churches was to be conducted, was part of his programme for enforcing conformity.

Laud's name is closely associated with that of Thomas Wentworth, Earl of Strafford. What Laud was to religion, Strafford was to civil government. As the King's chief minister in the later 1630s, Strafford conducted a policy of 'thorough', aiming to bring order and strong administration into the exercise of royal government. Laud and Strafford became objects of detestation to those who considered that religious and civil freedom was being destroyed by these policies. Despite the fact that they frightened most people, Laud and Strafford were beset by a major difficulty; they were strong men in a weak government. As events were to show, at crucial times they did not receive the backing of the King and court whom they were trying to serve.

The weakness of Charles's financial measures was that they could work only in peacetime when expenditure could be kept within bounds; they could not meet extraordinary demands on revenue. This became very evident in 1637. It was in that year that the government attempted to impose the Anglican Prayer Book on Scotland. The Scots, large numbers of whom were Presbyterians, rose in open rebellion. They deeply resented having their form of worship dictated to them by an English State Church. So serious was the rising that an English army had to be raised in an attempt to suppress it. This led to what became known as The Bishops' Wars, which lasted from 1637 to 1640. Armies are expensive, and Charles I was short of money. This forced him to recall Parliament in 1640 in order to ask it to grant him special subsidies to meet the cost of maintaining the English forces.

b) The Breakdown of Relations between King and Parliament, 1640–2

> **KEY ISSUE** What factors led to the outbreak of war between King and Parliament in 1642?

The very act of calling Parliament in April 1640 revealed that the King was in a desperate financial plight. This encouraged Parliament to go on the offensive. It refused to vote grants or supplies until its grievances over religion and taxation had been dealt with to its satisfaction. Angrily, the King dissolved this Parliament (later known as the Short Parliament) after only four weeks. But this merely made matters worse for Charles since he now had no means of raising the extra income he so badly needed. In the autumn the failures of the English army in Scotland obliged Charles to summon a new parliament. The scene was set for confrontation.

However, modern scholars have suggested that, at many points in 1640, matters might have been prevented from deteriorating into crisis had tact and foresight been shown by those involved. One example is the high-handed way in which the Privy Council (roughly equivalent to the modern Cabinet) negotiated with the Parliamentary leaders over money supply. The Council's approach was so dismissive that it prevented a workable compromise being reached. It is noteworthy that the Commons' assault on the royal policy was never directed at Charles himself. Members of Parliament were always careful to direct their attack at the corrupt ministers who had misled their monarch. This was not simply a formula for avoiding the taint of treason; it indicated that the opposition to royal policy was not intended as a challenge to monarchy itself. Charles I's majesty was not questioned. The changes that were being demanded were all regarded as falling within the existing constitutional structure. There was nothing revolutionary in intent in what the Commons did, although this is not to deny that it would be revolutionary in effect.

The Long Parliament (as it was to become known) met in an aggressive mood in November 1640. Its members believed that they had the government on the defensive. Led by John Pym, a staunch Presbyterian and a skilful parliamentary manager, the Commons organised themselves to attack the royal policy and assert the role of parliament as an essential part of the constitution. Shrewdly, Pym took as his first objective the bringing down of Strafford. He reasoned that if the chief architect of 'thorough', and by far the most able man in the King's service, could be removed, then the royal policy itself would collapse. Strafford was brought before Parliament on a charge of high treason. Despite offering a spirited defence, he was condemned and sentenced to death. Now occurred one of the decisive moments in the English Revolution. Would the King defend Strafford, whom he knew to be innocent, or would he sacrifice him as an act of appeasement to Parliament? He chose the latter course; he signed Strafford's death warrant. This, as Charles acknowledged at the time of his own execution eight years later, was an act of cowardice and betrayal.

'Black Tom is dead! Tyranny is dead!', the crowds shouted at the news of Strafford's beheading in May 1641. The way now seemed open for further encroachments on the royal power. The King's prerogative courts, Star Chamber and High Commission, were abolished and ship money was declared illegal. Acts were passed, requiring that Parliament be called at least once every three years, and outlawing its dissolution except by its own consent. In something of a daze, Charles, who had withdrawn to Scotland in May, gave his assent to all these measures, thus making them constitutional. Despite

Parliament's success in this, many MPs remained deeply fearful. They knew that all their gains might be swept away should the King choose to use his royal authority to dismiss Parliament by force of arms. There were constant rumours that this was the King's intention.

Matters took a dramatic turn in October 1641 with the outbreak of rebellion in Ireland (see page 28). Parliament's greatest anxiety was that if an army were to be raised to put down the Irish rebellion, it might first be used against them. In an effort to retain the initiative, the Commons issued the 'Grand Remonstrance', a document which listed all their political and religious grievances and contained the truly revolutionary demand that parliament should appoint the King's ministers. This was a demand too far for many MPs and caused a serious split in Parliament. The vote on the Remonstrance was carried by only 11 votes in the Commons and was not considered at all by the Lords. Parliamentary unanimity had broken down. Those who had previously been willing to see the limitation of royal power were now unhappy about the extreme steps that Parliament was contemplating. It was from this division that the two sides in the civil war – royalist and parliamentarian – would develop.

Religion was of critical importance in deepening the divide in Parliament. Those who believed that the Laudian repression and the Irish rebellion were part of a conspiracy to overthrow the Anglican Church and impose Popery in England looked to Parliament for protection. But many of those who earlier had been pleased to see restrictions placed on Laudianism now felt that things were being pushed too far. They became concerned that the Puritan anti-Laudians were beginning to use Parliament as the means of undermining the Anglican Church itself. This religious radicalism had been apparent in the 'Root and Branch Petition' of the autumn of 1640, which had attacked the episcopal system, and in the subsequent attempt of some parliamentarians to exclude the bishops from the House of Lords.

The King returned to London in November 1641, hoping to arouse support by playing on the divisions now appearing in Parliament. In a move to keep Charles on the defensive, the opposition faction in the Commons proposed impeaching the Queen, Henrietta Maria, on the grounds that she was plotting with the Irish rebels. Outraged by this charge, Charles decided at last to use force. In January 1642, he went in person with his guards to the Commons to arrest the five ringleaders behind the impeachment. However, they had been forewarned of the King's coming and, by the time he arrived at Westminster, they had been smuggled to safety. Charles had to withdraw empty-handed, amid angry members' cries of 'Privilege, privilege!'.

The King came very badly out of this incident. He had failed to arrest the five members but at the same time he had increased the fears of Parliament that he was preparing to crush opposition by military means. The London mob was encouraged to demonstrate in favour of Parliament. Fearing for his family's safety, Charles hurriedly left London to return to Scotland. On his journey north, he appealed to loyal subjects to rally to him.

Whether war was unavoidable at this point is still a major debating point, but certainly the two sides, as they may now be called, began to prepare for war. In March 1642, Parliament drew up a militia ordinance, giving it the right to levy troops. The King countered this in June by issuing commissions of array, which empowered his officials in the counties to raise forces. It was also in June that the Commons published the Nineteen Propositions. These called upon Charles to give over a whole range of royal powers to Parliament. His reply, issued in June, showed that he was not willing to go beyond the concessions he had granted in 1641. In August 1642, Charles raised his standard at Nottingham. The civil war had begun.

c) The First Civil War, 1642–6

> **KEY ISSUE** Why was Parliament able to defeat the King by 1646?

It is still common to refer to the Civil War as a struggle between King and Parliament, but it has to be remembered that these terms are a form of shorthand. They are useful but imprecise. Approximately one-third of the Commons supported the King in the war and two-thirds supported Parliament. In the House of Lords the proportions were reversed; two-thirds supported the King and one-third supported parliament. Thus as a body, Parliament was split in half diagonally. There was a similar division of support in the country at large; a rough line of demarcation ran from the north-east to the south-west, with parliament stronger to the south of that line and the royalists stronger to the north. This was by no means an exact division; there were pockets of resistance of a royalist or parliamentarian kind dotted throughout enemy territory.

The royalists had the better of the early stages of the war. This was due in part to the reluctance of the aristocratic leaders of the parliamentary forces, the Earl of Essex and the Earl of Manchester, to wage all-out war. Prominent among those parliamentarians who were angered by such lack of commitment was Oliver Cromwell. From his home base in East Anglia, Cromwell, hitherto a backbench MP, organised a force which eventually grew into the New Model Army. It quickly became renowned and feared for its discipline, religious zeal and fighting ability. Parliament, convinced that victory over the King could be achieved only if the dedication of the New Model was adopted by all their forces, persuaded the less resolute commanders to surrender their commissions. This was done by a ruse known as the Self-Denying Ordinance (1645), a Commons' resolution requiring serving officers to resign their positions and then seek re-appointment. The faint-hearts found that their commissions were not renewed. Their places were taken instead by the fully committed officers. Cromwell's New Model Army now became increasingly significant, politically as well as militarily, as the war continued.

Wars often have the effect of pushing those involved in directions that they had not originally planned to go. This was the case with the English Civil War. In order to gain military help, Parliament entered into the Solemn League and Covenant with the Scottish Presbyterians in 1643. In return for military support, Parliament promised to adopt Presbyterianism as the official religion of England. This was a highly significant development; Parliament in its anxiety to defeat the King had now formally committed itself to replacing one form of state religion, Anglicanism, with another, Presbyterianism. Those parliamentarians who had taken up arms against the King in order to be free of an established church saw the Solemn League and Covenant as a betrayal.

The move also caused a major shift in the relations between Parliament and the army, and marked an important stage in the emergence of the latter as a political and religious force. As the war progressed, the Parliamentary army came increasingly to represent the Protestant sects who wanted freedom of worship for individual congregations without control by a centralised state church. This development ran counter to the trend in the Commons. There, as the signing of the Solemn League and Covenant showed, the upper hand had been gained by those MPs who wanted the replacement of the Laudian Anglican Church with the Presbyterian state model. A critical divergence of attitude had begun to develop between Parliament and its own army.

By 1646, Parliament's greater economic resources, its control of the major ports, and its possession of London, the nation's administrative and financial capital, had brought it victory. Militarily, the extraordinary abilities of Oliver Cromwell, who had not taken up arms until he was over forty, proved the major factor in the defeat of the royalists. Despite the brilliance of individual commanders, the King's army could not match the New Model in ability, organisation and resolve.

d) The Failure to Reach a Settlement, 1646–9

> **KEY ISSUE** Why was there a second civil war in 1648?

In many ways, the defeat of the King in 1646 left the political situation more uncertain than when war had broken out four years earlier. Parliament was now divided between the Presbyterians and the 'Independents', the spokesmen of the Protestant sects. The Presbyterian element in the Commons pressed for the disbanding of the army as soon as hostilities were over, but the rank and file soldiers in the infantry and cavalry, supported by their officers, refused to do so until their arrears of pay had been met and they had received a guarantee they would not be prosecuted for deeds done during the war. In 1647 the army marched on London in a show of force.

It was the attitude of Charles I that prevented a political settlement being reached after the war ended in 1646. His defeat had not destroyed kingship. He believed he had suffered nothing more than a military reverse. Between 1646 and 1648 Charles entered into negotiations with all the major groups – Parliament, the army, and the Scots – with a view to restoring his authority. He played the groups off against each other and made contradictory promises that he did not intend to keep. That was why all attempts to find 'an accommodation with his Majesty' eventually broke down. One of Charles's promises led directly to the outbreak of the Second Civil War in 1648. Late in 1647, the King entered into an 'Engagement' with the Scots in which he promised to do what the English parliament had reneged upon, to adopt Presbyterianism as the official form of church worship. This was almost a complete reversal of the alignment of 1642. Whereas the first civil war had been Parliament and Scots against the King, the second civil war was King and Scots against Parliament.

In the struggle that followed, the Scots and the English royalists failed to co-ordinate their plans effectively. This, and the speed at which the army under Fairfax and Cromwell responded, made Charles I's cause a hopeless one militarily. The royalists experienced a crushing defeat. The completeness of the King's failure reinforced a powerful feeling among the army and some of the MPs that he was personally responsible for all the bloodshed and misery suffered by the kingdom since 1642. The General Council of the Army decided that Charles must be removed. However, they resolved that this would not be done 'in a hole and corner manner', but by putting him on public trial. The army wished to clothe its actions in legal form. Modern historians have stressed how important this is as an illustration of how far the army was from contemplating revolution.

To prepare for the trial, the General Council took steps to debar from Parliament all those MPs who were likely to oppose the plan for bringing the King to account. In December 1648, Colonel Pride, acting on behalf of the Army Council, stood at the door of the Commons and forcibly turned away those members, mainly Presbyterians, who were known to favour continued negotiations with the King. This event has become known as 'Pride's Purge'. Those MPs who remained in the Commons after the Purge became known collectively as the Rump.

Yet again, circumstances had forced people of influence into making decisions and taking steps that they would not have contemplated earlier. The climax of this came with the trial and execution of the King in January 1649. Although it was dressed in legal forms and justified by arguments of principle, the King's execution marked the culmination of ten years of political failure.

e) The Trial and Execution of the King, 1649

> **KEY ISSUES** Was the trial of Charles I legal?
> Did Parliament have any alternative but to execute the King?

To give themselves the authority to try the King, the Commons asserted early in January 1649 that 'the supreme power in this nation' was now vested solely in them, without the need of King or House of Lords. At the trial, the High Court, specially created by the Rump to prosecute the King, claimed to represent the will of 'the people of England', against whom the King had offended. This claim, which flew in the face of all precedent and law, was the Rump's weakest point. When the charge was read out, impeaching the King in the name 'of the people of England', a woman in the gallery cried out: 'No, nor the hundredth part of them'. The rumour was that she was Lady Fairfax, the wife of the commander of Parliament's army, a sign of how deeply the King's trial had divided the nation.

The trial was in no sense an impartial attempt to establish Charles's guilt or innocence. It was a show trial; his guilt was assumed from the beginning. This had been evident at the outbreak of the second civil war in May 1648 when the army had declared its intention 'to call Charles Stuart, that man of blood, to an account for the blood he had shed'.

Against expectation, Charles conducted himself well at his trial. He behaved with dignity and lost the stammer that had habitually handicapped his public speaking. He refused to recognise the court or to plead, but took the opportunity, when permitted to speak, to ask his accusers by what legal authority they brought him before them. It was the one question to which they had no legitimate answer. He had a case grounded in law and tradition that the hastily-created High Court could not match. He rejected the whole proceedings on the grounds that 'a king cannot be tried by any superior jurisdiction on earth'. Whatever Charles's personal responsibility may have been for the civil wars, there is no doubt that he had the better of the argument at his trial. However, his fate had been pre-determined. He was declared guilty and condemned to death by beheading. On 30 January 1649, the sentence was carried out.

The next logical step was for the Rump to abolish both the monarchy and the Lords. This was formally done in March 1649, but only after considerable debate about whether it was the right course. The delay and uncertainty suggests how far from being truly revolutionary the Rump actually was. Of course, in one sense there are few things more revolutionary than the beheading of a reigning monarch, but it has to be re-emphasised that Charles's execution was not undertaken primarily in order to bring about a constitutional change. It was foremost a remedy for the insoluble problem of what to do with a defeated king who would not accept his defeat. Republicanism had never been very strong in England. The civil wars had been fought not to destroy kingship but to limit its powers. The decision to put Charles on trial was made very late in the struggle between King and Parliament. It was an act of desperation that arose from the impossibility of negotiating with him. The members of the purged Parliament and of the army who voted for the King's trial and execution had decided reluctantly that there was no alternative to his permanent removal.

The majority of the people in Britain were shocked by the sacrilege that the execution of an anointed monarch represented. The strength of this feeling was shown by the large number of Charles's opponents who, no matter how much they blamed him for the nation's sufferings, could not bring themselves to be involved in his judicial murder. However, for the regicides (those who signed his death warrant) it was a duty they had to fulfil. Charles was a man 'against whom the Lord himself hath witnessed'. Cromwell is reputed to have said at the time that 'we will cut off his head with the crown upon it' and that the execution was a 'cruel necessity'. There is no hard evidence that he said either of these things, but their sentiment accurately expressed the attitude of the regicides in 1649.

2 The Interregnum, 1649–60

> **KEY ISSUE** What were the basic difficulties facing the various governments during the period of the Interregnum?

These 12 years were taken up with a continual effort to establish a stable constitution to replace the monarchy that had been abolished in 1649. Between 1649 and 1653, England was a Commonwealth, ruled by a Council of State appointed by Parliament, which was itself the purged remnant of the Long Parliament first called in 1640. In 1653, Oliver Cromwell, the head of the army, forcibly dissolved this 'Rump' Parliament. This was soon followed by the establishment of a Protectorate with Cromwell as Lord Protector, a position he held until his death five years later in 1658. In one obvious sense, Cromwell was a military dictator, but this was not his intention. He experimented with various forms of parliament, always with the intention of returning England to civilian government. The dilemma which he was never able to resolve was that, whatever form of constitution was adopted, its security could be guaranteed only by the support of the military. At his death in 1658, the army still held the key to any settlement. This was shown when, after two years of political confusion which included the unsuccessful attempt of Cromwell's son, Richard,

Charles I's death warrant. Cromwell's signature is the third down in the far left column to carry on the Protectorate, the army played the central role in bringing about the restoration of the Stuart monarchy.

The Interregnum may be described, therefore, as a time when those in power sought to establish a form of government which possessed the stability and acceptability of the pre-1640 political system. With the various experiments to achieve the desired constitutional balance all proving unsuccessful, the only logical course was a return to kingship, which, with all its previous shortcomings, was deemed superior to any of the attempts to replace it. But it must be remembered that this description simplifies what was a much more complex process. It does not explain, for example, the existence of the radical social and religious movements of the period. Nonetheless, it does remain a useful broad frame of reference by which to begin analysing the Interregnum.

3 Historians and the Interregnum

> **KEY ISSUE** What was the historical importance of the Interregnum?

For a number of decades after the Second World War, the Marxist view of history dominated the interpretations of the English Revolution. There was a strong tendency to view the events of 1640–60 as a class struggle, in which economic factors pre-determined how the political situation would develop. The crises and conflicts that produced the Civil War could be properly understood only if they were set in the broader pattern of social and economic change. The leading representative of this approach was Christopher Hill, acknowledged by all scholars, whatever their own leanings, as an outstanding scholar whose prolific writings have illuminated our understanding of seventeeth-century Britain.[1]

In more recent years, studies of the period have been strongly influenced by revisionist ideas. This has led to a shift of emphasis. There has been a tendency to dismiss the concept of class-conflict as the major dynamic behind events and to suggest instead that the struggle is better understood as the product of political failure. Many modern scholars, of whom Conrad Russell and Derek Hirst are outstanding examples, stress that the struggle between King and Parliament was largely brought about by political mistakes and personal errors.[2] They do not deny that there were long-term causes of the troubles, but they argue that these did not make a conflict inevitable. They suggest that, if Charles I had been of a different temperament or if he had shown greater political skills, the civil wars and all that followed might have been avoided. This is a corrective to the view that the English Revolution was the climax of a century of social and economic developments that led inexorably to a final struggle for power.

Revisionists warn against reading history backwards or being too impressed by the radical ideas of the time as if these anticipated such later notions as socialism, popular sovereignty and parliamentary democracy. They lay weight on the predominantly conservative aims of those involved in the events of the period; it was a revolution without revolutionaries. According to this interpretation, the period 1640–9 saw individuals and groups being forced by circumstances into going further than they had originally intended. The following period, 1649–60, then witnessed a succession of attempts to make the new situation work. This ultimately failed because those who held power were unable to reconcile the new political and religious order with their own innate conservatism. They then judged that the only way to ensure stability and security, which had been their objective in taking up arms against the King in the first place, was by a return to monarchy.

Another important feature of current historiography is the weight given to Irish and Scottish affairs. Historians are now anxious that England should not be considered in isolation; it was one part of the three kingdoms over which the Stuarts ruled. Ronald Hutton has reminded us that we should consider Britain as a whole when we examine the so-called English Revolution.[3] He was careful to call his book on the Interregnum, *The British Republic 1649–60*, for it was during the years of the republic that Ireland and Scotland were politically subjugated to England, producing a situation that largely determined the character of Britain from that time onward.

A further consideration of note is that most books generalise when they describe the developments within this period. They tend to concentrate on central and national developments rather than on what was happening locally. This is not a failing. It is in some ways unavoidable. Writers do not have unlimited space; unless they generalise, they cannot give a broad picture or unravel complicated affairs. However, we do need to be reminded that, for every general statement that is made, there are probably many exceptions. This observation is particularly relevant to the history of the local communities in this period. The pioneering studies of Alan Everitt into local history have been carried on by teams of scholars whose researches have led to important shifts of emphasis and interpretation of the period overall. John Morrill, Ann Hughes and David Underdown have all made valuable contributions in this area.[4]

The figure of Oliver Cromwell overshadows the whole of the Interregnum and he continues to fascinate the observer. Whether this God-obsessed man and peerless general was genuinely seeking the spiritual regeneration of the nation through religious reformation or whether he was a calculating politician intent on gaining and holding personal power are questions over which scholars and biographers continue to disagree. For centuries after his death it was common for him to be regarded as a 'brave bad man', the description given him by the contemporary royalist chronicler, the Earl of Clarendon. Few historians now would be so confident in their definitions. What attracts their attention is the intriguing personal psychology that shaped Cromwell's religious and political outlook and motivated his actions.

Remarkable though Cromwell was, it may well be that his role during the Interregnum has been exaggerated in the past. Recent research has indicated that the Protectorate governments never exercised the degree of centralised control often ascribed to them. Barry Coward, one of Cromwell's major biographers, has supported those local historians who have pointed out that many of the administrative policies pursued in the 1650s were initiated and shaped at local not national level.[5]

The Interregnum is very much a paradox. Between 1649 and 1660 a series of successive regimes, which owed their existence to a revolution but which in character and attitude were overwhelmingly conservative, sought to restore a stable traditional constitution. This creates a danger that the Restoration of 1660 will be seen as having been inevitable and the period from 1649 to 1660 as simply a series of failed experiments that led, step by step, to the return of monarchy. Inevitability is a dangerous concept, which historians are reluctant to apply to the events they study. Moreover, even if it were the case that the restoration was unavoidable, it would still be important to discover why this was so.

There are a number of features of the Interregnum that have proved of long-term historical significance. John Morrill has gone as far as to claim that, 'we are the product of a history which has left a residue of the traumas of the 1650s in our national psyche'.[6] In the 1650s, Scotland and Ireland were brought directly under English rule, making it possible for the first time to speak of 'Britain' as a political entity. Never before had the nation experienced the commanding presence of a standing army in times of peace. At no point had England's reputation as a military power stood so high abroad. For the only time in its history, England tried to govern itself without a monarch, but with a single chamber parliament and a written constitution. It is true that this experiment was presided over for the greater part of the time by a Protector whose authority rested on his military power, but this serves to re-emphasise the extraordinary character of the period and also to explain the interests that it holds for historians.

What modern analysts increasingly stress is that the real historical importance of the Interregnum is to be found in its negative aspects. David L. Smith has observed: 'The years 1649–60 still mark an aberration in English constitutional history ... Yet it is precisely this fact which makes the Interregnum so important. Its long-term significance lies not in what it created but in what it *discredited*.'[7] The lesson of the period was that, despite valiant and desperate efforts to prove the contrary, the only workable alternative to monarchy was rule by the military. It was an alternative that very few wanted.

References

1 E.g., Christopher Hill, *The Century of Revolution 1603–1714*, Nelson, 1961.
2 E.g., Conrad Russell, *The Crisis of Parliaments in English History 1509–60*, OUP, 1982 and Derek Hirst, *England in Conflict 1603–1660*, Hodder Headline, 1999.
3 Ronald Hutton, *The British Republic 1649–60*, Macmillan, 1990.
4 Alan Everitt, *The Community of Kent and the Great Rebellion*, Historical Association, 1966; John Morrill, *Cheshire 1630–60*, Oxford, 1974; Ann Hughes, *Politics, Society and Civil War in Warwickshire, 1620–1660*, Cambridge, 1987; David Underdown, *Revel, Riot and Rebellion – Popular Politics in England 1603–1660*, OUP, 1985.
5 Barry Coward, *Oliver Cromwell*, Longman, 1991.
6 John Morrill, *Revolution and Restoration: England in the 1650s*, Collins and Brown, 1992. p. 7.
7 David L. Smith, 'The Struggle for New Constitutional and Institutional Forms', in John Morrill (Ed.), *Revolution and Restoration: England in the 1650s*, Collins and Brown, 1992, pp. 32–33.

Working on Chapter I

No historical period can be fully understood without reference to the time that preceded it. This is especially true of the Interregnum, since it was in all major respects a reaction to what had occurred between 1637 and 1649, the period of the English Revolution. It is important, therefore, when studying the Interregnum to be aware of the main political, religious and military developments that constituted the Revolution. Your aim, therefore, in reading this chapter should be twofold: to grasp the essential developments that took place between 1637 and 1649, and to gain an outline knowledge of the key aspects of the Interregnum that followed. One of the attractions of the Interregnum as a period of study is that it can be broken down logically into neat compartments, such as 'Commonwealth', 'Protectorate', 'foreign policy', 'Cromwell', and 'Restoration'. These obviously overlap and interconnect at many points, but it is possible to study each of them as a distinct topic. That is the approach followed in this book.

Summary Diagram
The Interregnum: an Introduction

the English Revolution, 1640–9

|

the prelude
the policy of 'thorough'– Laud and Strafford, 1629–40
the Bishops' Wars, 1637–40

|

the breakdown
King and Parliament, 1640–2

|

the First Civil War 1642–6
the entry of the Scots
the Solemn League and Covenant, 1643
Cromwell and the New Model Army
the royalists defeated by 1646

the failure to reach a settlement, 1646–8
the Leveller movement, 1647
the Second Civil War, 1648
royalists again defeated, 1648
Pride's Purge, 1648
the trial and execution of the King, 1649

THE INTERREGNUM

the Commonwealth, 1649–53

|

the Protectorate of Oliver Cromwell, 1653–8

|

the Protectorate of Richard Cromwell, 1658–9

|

the path to Restoration, 1659–60

|

the Interregnum in perspective

2 The Rump Parliament, 1649–53

POINTS TO CONSIDER

The execution of Charles I created more problems than it solved. It left England facing a series of demanding questions. How would it govern itself without a king? How would it tackle the deeply troublesome political, religious and social issues that the civil wars had left unresolved? Who now held the real power in the land – Parliament or the army? The major developments of the years 1649–53, the period when the Rump Parliament tried to establish itself as the legitimate authority in the new republic, are the subjects of this chapter. Your task is to study the separate sections in sequence. This will provide you with an understanding of the strained relations between the Rump and its army and an appreciation of the challenges presented by the Leveller movement in England and by the rebellions in Ireland and Scotland. You need to pay particular attention to Oliver Cromwell's policies in Ireland since debate still rages over these. The chapter concludes with an assessment of the Rump's achievements and failures. You can use this section as a starting point for your own assessment of the record of the Rump Parliament.

KEY DATES

1648	**Dec**	Pride's Purge.
1649	**Jan**	Trial and execution of Charles I.
		Commons claimed 'supreme power'.
	Feb	Charles II proclaimed King in Scotland.
		Council of State appointed.
	Mar	Rump abolished the monarchy and the House of Lords.
		Cromwell appointed Lord Lieutenant in charge of Parliament's army.
	Apr	Digger commune set up in Surrey.
	May	England declared to be a Commonwealth.
		Leveller rising against Rump crushed by Cromwell.
	Aug	Cromwell landed in Ireland.
	Sept	Siege of Drogheda.
	Oct	Siege of Wexford.
1650	**Jan**	Engagement Act.
	May	Rump recalled Cromwell to England.
	June	Cromwell replaced Fairfax as Commander-in-Chief.
	July	Treason Act.
	Aug	Blasphemy Act.
		Cromwell entered Scotland.
		Cromwell's victory over Scots at Dunbar.

1651	Jan	Charles II crowned in Scotland.
	Sept	Cromwell defeated Charles II at Worcester.
	Oct	Navigation Act introduced.
		Charles II escaped to France.
1652	May	Outbreak of the Dutch War.
	July	Fleetwood became Commander-in-Chief in Ireland.
	Aug	Settlement of Ireland Act began the Cromwellian land confiscation.
		Committee for the Propagation of the Gospel formed.
1653	Apr	Rump forcibly dispersed by Cromwell.

1 The Rump and the Army

> **KEY ISSUE** How dependent was the Rump on the army between 1649 and 1653?

It had been on the orders of the General Council of the Army that Colonel Pride had carried out his purge of the Long Parliament in December 1648. The General Council had no constitutional authority, but circumstances had made it a formidable political force. It was well represented in Parliament since a large number of the army officers were also MPs, Oliver Cromwell being the most notable example. The undeniable fact was that the Rump had been brought into being by the army and could never forget that its continued existence depended on the willingness of the military to support it. This put the General Council in a powerful position. If it chose to insist on a certain policy or course of action, it would be difficult for the Rump to resist it, let alone ignore it. Thus, although in theory the army after 1648 continued as the servant of parliament, in reality the relationship had been reversed.

Both Thomas Fairfax (Lord General of the Army) and Oliver Cromwell (Lieutenant-General, in charge of the cavalry) had been slow to accept the necessity of the King's trial. Cromwell, far from being the initiator of events, did not return to London until after Pride's Purge had taken place. Indeed, it is likely that he deliberately delayed his return in order to avoid having to make a decision. For about three weeks after the Purge he appears to have believed that a settlement with Charles was still possible. However, as was invariably the case with Cromwell, once he had made up his mind he acted in a totally resolute manner, as if all doubts had fled. This was an aspect of his belief that it was God who directly guided his judgements.

There is little doubt that by 1649 Oliver Cromwell's great military successes and his involvement in the removal of the King had made him a powerful figure. But it is important to emphasise that at this stage he held no formal position that conferred authority on him. As a soldier, he was technically still the servant of Parliament, and was subordinate to Lord Fairfax. However, since Fairfax had chosen, by 1649, to withdraw from public affairs, Cromwell became increasingly important politically. His rise to prominence is an example of how in times of uncertainty it is actual rather than theoretical power that matters. Whatever parliamentarians might claim to the contrary, the army was the real power in the land. As a consequence, Cromwell, the effective leader of the army, became the dominant figure in the nation. Although this did not mean he was all-powerful – he never became that – it did mean that his actions were critical in determining how the political situation developed.

Pride's Purge had reduced the House of Commons from 470 members to 211. But this remnant was not a united body. Only 70 of them had been involved in the setting up of the High Court that had tried the King, and of that number only 43 members had signed his death warrant. This suggests that Pride's Purge had not reduced Parliament to being simply the mouthpiece of the army, and it soon became clear that the Rump did not regard itself as dependent on the army for its authority. It claimed to be the legitimate continuation of the Long Parliament, elected in 1640, and, therefore, entitled to the loyalty and obedience of the whole nation, including the army. It was a hollow claim. The truth was that the Rump existed as the result of a military purge, a fact that compromised its authority throughout its four years of government.

This is not to argue that England was under direct military rule after Pride's Purge. Modern historians have emphasised what a remarkably restrained body the army was. Although the radical group, the Levellers, were influential in the ranks after 1647 (see page 21), they were very much a minority and were restricted to certain regiments. The army in its entirety never became radicalised. It was always under the control of the Army Council, the body which, since the formation of the New Model during the First Civil War, had been responsible for forming military policy and directing the troops. The Army Council was composed of the highest-ranking officers, often referred to as 'Grandees'. They were men of good birth, such as Fairfax, or of property, such as Cromwell, who certainly did not want further political or social upheaval. Indeed, rather than a military takeover, Pride's Purge may be interpreted as an example of the army's moderation in that it wished to retain the essential elements of constitutional government. The Army Council had resisted those who had urged a total dispersal of the Long Parliament and the appointment of an entirely new legislature.

2 The Establishment of the Commonwealth

> **KEY ISSUE** What principles underlay the creation of the Commonwealth?

In the statute of 13 February 1649, which set up a Council of State to act as the government, England was defined as a 'Commonwealth'. This was confirmed in May by an Act declaring England to be a 'Commonwealth and Free State'. The first Council of State was composed of 41 members, 34 of whom were MPs. Its composition reflected the conservatism of the Rump. It was successful in preventing a number of influential officers, including Henry Ireton and Thomas Harrison, the leader of the Fifth Monarchists (see page 71), from being voted onto the Council.

The Rump certainly did not intend the abolition of monarchy and the declaration of a Commonwealth to be the prelude to a revolution. These measures were meant to consolidate what had been achieved by the defeat of the royalists in the civil wars. The Rump's purpose was to preserve rather than to undermine the constitution. Charles I, it was claimed, had tried to subvert the fundamental laws of the kingdom and impose a tyranny. That was why it had been necessary to remove him. As for the House of Lords, the argument was that, by making no effort to prevent royal oppression, it had ceased to play its proper constitutional role. Moreover, since its numbers had dwindled to a mere handful, it was clearly no longer of any practical value.

However, not all MPs thought along these lines. Cromwell wondered whether there was not a case for keeping an upper house. He warned the Rump that it would be short-sighted 'to take these courses to incense the peers against them when they had more need to study a near union with them'. His views appear to have been shaped by his wish to preserve good relations with the aristocracy. Although he subsequently accepted the abolition of the Lords, Cromwell provided further evidence of his conservatism when he persuaded the Rump to substitute a milder oath of loyalty to the new regime for the one originally drafted. The first form of the oath had required those joining the Council of State to recognise the validity of Pride's purge and the King's execution. Cromwell's compromise version merely required the Councillors to declare their loyalty to 'the present parliament in the maintenance and defence of the public liberty of the nation'.

This concession eased the way for those who had earlier been unwilling to approve of the Purge and the King's trial. They could now openly accept the new Commonwealth. David Underdown has stressed the significance of this: 'by encouraging as many MPs as possible to align themselves with the Commonwealth, even if in their hearts they did not believe in it, the original Rumpers themselves hoped to destroy what impetus the revolution possessed'.[1] The conservatism of the Rump disappointed and embittered those radicals who had expected Charles I's execution and the creation of the Commonwealth to be the prelude to a social and religious reformation. The most immediate radical challenge to the new order of things came from the Levellers.

3 The Challenge of the Levellers

> **KEY ISSUES** How serious a threat to the Rump were the Levellers?
> Why did the Leveller movement fail to achieve its main objectives?

a) Background

The Leveller movement was one of the most remarkable political developments to grow out of the English Revolution. It had begun in London during the first civil war among the 'middling sort' of civilians, such as shop-keepers and tradesmen, and soon became influential in a number of army regiments. The basic principle of the Levellers was that sovereignty lay not with Parliament but with the people. They demanded the extension of the parliamentary franchise, reform of the legal system, and the recognition of certain fundamental rights, including freedom of worship.

These socially disruptive ideas were unacceptable to the Grandees, the conservative-minded senior army officers. However, between 1647 and 1649, it had served the interests of the Grandees to appear to go along with some of the Leveller demands. This had been done in order to preserve the loyalty of the rank and file during the troubled years of political realignment that led to the second civil war. In 1647 the Grandees had incorporated into their proposals for a settlement with the King, a number of clauses from the Leveller document, the *Agreement of the People*. This was a matter of expediency; the Grandees had no basic sympathy with Leveller ideas. This had been apparent in the sharp clashes in the army debates that had been held at Putney in 1647 and at Windsor in 1648 when the Grandees had rejected the claim of the rank and file that the right to vote should no longer be restricted to property holders. Moreover, when Leveller-inspired mutinies had broken out in 1648, Cromwell had moved promptly and firmly to suppress them.

b) Lilburne and Cromwell

In the winter of 1648–9, at the time of Pride's Purge and the King's trial, when the Army Council was anxious to maintain army unity, the Levellers seemed again to be influential. But, as earlier, this proved illusory. The new Commonwealth that was established after Charles I's execution was in no respect a concession to Leveller demands. John Lilburne, the leading Leveller, was quick to recognise this. In February 1649 he published a withering attack on the Rump. His main charge was well expressed in the title of his pamphlet, *England's New Chains Discovered*. He denounced the Rump for seizing power from the people and condemned the Council of State as an unelected clique to whom the people of England owed neither loyalty nor obedience. In another pamphlet, he accused Cromwell of high treason for his part in the King's execution. Such defiance could not be tolerated; Lilburne and three fellow-pamphleteers were arrested and brought before the Council of State, which committed them to the Tower of London.

Lilburne's defiance helped to inspire resistance in the ranks of the army. Dislike of the Rump, combined with the soldiers' fear of being sent to Ireland with their arrears unpaid, led to a rash of protests, including the re-publication of the *Agreement of the People*. In May a number of units mutinied. Cromwell was instructed by the Rump to crush this rising. He needed little urging. Lilburne in his account of his interrogation by the Council of State recorded Cromwell as saying of the Levellers:

> 1   I tell you, you have no other way to deal with these men but to break them, or they will break you; yea, and bring all the guilt and blood and treasure shed and spent in this kingdom upon your heads and shoulders, and frustrate and make void all that work that, with so many
> 5   years' industry, toil and pain you have done, and so render you to all rational men in the world as the most contemptiblest generation of silly, low-spirited men in the earth, to be broken and routed by such a despicable, contemptible generation of men as they are.[2]

Cromwell's severity, and the speed with which he moved against the Levellers in 1649, illustrated his determination to win support for the Commonwealth from the traditional governing classes by proving that the new regime would not tolerate social disruption. Having assured the loyal regiments of the Rump's intention to settle their arrears of pay, he appealed for their assistance in subduing 'the army revolters which are now called by the name of Levellers'. Then he and Fairfax chased the retreating Levellers across two counties before cornering them at Burford in Oxfordshire on 14 May. After a token resistance, the mutineers surrendered; they were court-martialled, and three of their ringleaders were shot. This, together with the overwhelming of two mutinous troops of cavalry in Northamptonshire two days later, marked the end of the Leveller rising in the army. It also meant, in effect, the end of the Leveller movement as a political force in the country at large.

JOHN LILBURNE

-Profile-

1614	born
1630	became an apprenticed cloth worker
1638–40	imprisoned by Star Chamber for his anti-government pamphlets
1642–5	fought as a soldier for Parliament
1645	refused to sign the Covenant and withdrew from the war
1646	imprisoned for challenging the authority of the Presbyterian-dominated Parliament
1648	released
1649	opposed Cromwell and the regicides tried for sedition
1649–51	became a prominent figure in the Leveller resistance to the Rump
1652	banished from England by the Rump
1653	tried for sedition
1653–5	held in prison
1655	became a Quaker
1657	died

A natural rebel and trouble-maker, John Lilburne was a constant thorn in the side of the authorities. Throughout his life he retained a deep distrust of those who wielded power, whether they were kings, bishops, generals, parliaments or protectors. In the late 1630s he suffered a series of severe punishments at the hands of Star Chamber for his opposition to Charles I's 'tyranny'. His self-belief and courage enabled him to endure being flogged, pilloried and imprisoned. His unbreakable spirit earned him the popular title of 'free-born John'. Released from prison by the Long Parliament, he took up arms against the royalists during the first civil war. He was captured in 1643 but later released in an exchange of prisoners. As the war developed, he grew alarmed at the growing strength of the Presbyterians and refused to fight for Parliament after 1645. He became equally disturbed by the emergence of the army leaders as a political force. In 1649, he launced a bitter pamphlet war against Cromwell and the Army Council. He denied that the Rump had the right to try Charles I and was outraged by what he regarded as its usurping of authority following the execution of the King. For this, he was tried for sedition but acquitted. An interesting development had occurred while he had been in prison. His wife, Elizabeth, took up his cause. She organised a petition demanding her husband's release, which was eventually signed by 10,000 women.

Despite Cromwell's crushing of the Levellers in 1649, Lilburne continued to attack the Rump as an unlawful and ungodly body. He directed particular venom at the commercial interests, such as the merchant monopoly companies, which he accused as profiteering under the new republic. Fierce retaliation from the republicans in the Rump, among whom Arthur Haselrig was the most prominent, resulted in Lilburne being formally banished from England. However, after leaving for Holland in 1652, he returned a year later. He was re-arrested and again charged with sedition. Once more he was acquitted to great popular acclaim. It was said that the shouts that went up from the crowd when the jury declared him not guilty could be heard over a mile away. But 'free-born' John was too disruptive a figure to be allowed to go entirely free. Under the pretext that he was still under banishment, he was held in a variety of prisons until 1655 when he was released on becoming a Quaker. He had two more years to live; during that time he devoted himself to writing religious works.

c) The Failure of the Levellers

The question arises as to why a movement which had seemed so powerful only a short time before should have been so easily crushed. There are several explanations. One is that the Leveller movement proved weaker than it appeared. In 1649 it was little more than three years old, far too short a time for it to have taken root in English society. The Leveller leaders, such as Lilburne, Overton and Walwyn, were effective propagandists, and attracted considerable attention. But attention does not necessarily mean support. We now know that the Leveller 'agitators' in the ranks had very limited success. For example, they were never able to persuade more than a small minority of the army units to follow them into open defiance of authority. Out of an army of 40,000, barely 800 soldiers joined the revolt in May 1649. The truth was that although the army rank and file had certainly become politicised since 1647, they had not become radicalised. The troops were primarily concerned with gaining better pay and conditions of service. When Cromwell and Ireton persuaded the Rump in 1649 to provide the back-pay owed to the soldiers, unrest in the ranks was greatly reduced.

AN IMPEACHMENT
OF
HIGH TREASON
AGAINST

Oliver Cromwel, and his Son in Law *Henry Ireton* Esquires, late Members of the late forcibly diffolved Houfe of Commons, prefented to publique view ; by *Lieutenant Colonel Iohn Lilburn* clofe Prifoner in rhe Tower of London , for his real, true and zealous affections to the Liberties of his native Country.

In which following Difcourfe or Impeachment, he engageth upon his life, either upon the principles of Law (*by way of indictment, the only and alone legall way of all ryals in England*) or upon the principles of Parliaments ancient proceedings, or upon the principles of reafon (*by pretence of which alone, they lately took away the Kings life*) before a legal Magiftracy, when there fhal be one again in England (*which now in the leaft there is not*) to prove the faid *Oliver Cromwel* guilty of the higheft Treafon that ever was acted in England, and more deferving punifhment and death.

Then the 44 Judges hanged for injuftice by *King Alfred* before the Conqueft ; or then the Lord *chief Juftice Wayland* and his affociates tormented by *Edw.* 1. Or, then Judg *Thorpe*, condemned to dye for Bribery in *Edw.* 3. time ; Or, then the *two dif-throned Kings Edw.* 2. *and Rich.* 2. Or, then the Lord chief Juftice *Trefillian*, (*who had His throat cut at Tyburn as a Traitor in Rich.* 2. *time, for fubverting the Law*) and all his affociates ; Or, then thofe two grand Traytorly fubverters of the Laws and Liberties of England, *Empfon* and *Dudley*, who therefore as Traytors loft their heads upon Tower-hill, in the beginning of *Henr.* 8. raign ; Or, then trayterous Cardinal *Wolfey*, who after he was arrefted of Treafon, poyfoned himfelf ; Or, then the late trayterous *Ship-Money Judges*, who with one Verdict or Judgment deftroyed all our propertie ; Or, then the late trayterous Bifhop of *Canterbury*, Earl of *Strafford*, Lord-Keeper *Finch*, Secretary *Windebanck*, or then Sir *George Ratcliff*, or all his Affociates ; Or, then the two *Hothams*, who loft their heads for correfponding with the Queen, &c ; Or, then the late King *Charls* whom themfelves have beheaded for a *Tyrant* and *traytor*.

In which are alfo fome Hints of Cautions to the Lord FAIRFAX, for abfolutely *breaking his folemn Engagement with his fouldiers, &c.* to take head and to regain his loft Credit in acting honeftly in time to come; in helping to fettle the Peace and Liberties of the Nation, which truly, really, and laftingly can never be done, but *by eftablifhing the principles of the Agreement of the Free People*; that being really the peoples intereft, and all the reft that went before, but particular and fly ih.

In which is alfo the Authors late Propofition fent to Mr *Holland*, June 26. 1649. to juftifie and make good at his utmeft hazard (upon the principles of *Scrip* re, Law, Reafon, and the *Parliaments and Armies anceint Declarations*) his late actions or writings in any or all his Books.

Ier. 6, 27, 8, 29. *For among my people are found wicked men : they lye in wait as he that fetteth fnares, th fet a trap, they catch men. As a cage is full of Birds, fo are their houfes full of deceit ; therefore they are become great, and waxen rich. They are waxen fat, they fhine; yea, they overpafs the deeds of the wicked; they j dg not the caufe, the caufe of th Fatherlefs, yet they profper; and the right of the needy doe they not j dg. Shall I not vifit for thefe things, faith the Lord ? Shall not my foul be avenged of fuch a Nation as tha ?*

The first page of Lilburne's pamphlet impeaching Cromwell

Another explanation is that by 1649 the conditions which had given the Levellers such strength as they had possessed had changed. There had been occasions during the previous two years when the turmoil of the times had encouraged the spread of Leveller ideas. The failure to reach a settlement with the King and the disruption of the second civil war had created an unstable situation, made worse by the economic depression of the late 1640s when poor harvests had led to bread shortages and high prices. Such conditions made Leveller arguments appear attractive as a means of protesting against the grimness of the prevailing conditions. But when better times returned in 1649, in the form of improved harvests, lower prices and higher wages, the Levellers had less fertile ground for sowing dissension.

A particular weakness of the Levellers was that they gained very few adherents among the army officers. Although, on occasion, the Grandees were prepared to enter into debate with the Levellers, they were unwilling to forego their natural conservatism by actively supporting a group of social radicals. The inability of the Leveller movement to make headway among the officers was matched by its failure to gain substantial support in Parliament, either before or after Pride's Purge. With the exception of Henry Marten, a committed republican, no influential parliamentarian publicly sympathised with the Levellers. This failure to win backing among the highest echelons of army and Parliament denied the Levellers an effective power base. A similar limitation applied geographically. At no time, outside London and parts of the south-east, did the movement command regular support.

It is also true that the Levellers never really produced a co-ordinated programme of action for changing society. Certainly, the *Agreement of the People* and *England's New Chains Discovered* expressed striking ideas, but these did not amount to a practical alternative constitution. They were essentially outbursts of frustration at the political and social imbalance which allowed, first, a royal despotism and, then, a parliamentary one to operate in England.

The Levellers' threat to the traditional social balance and order frightened the men of property. The weight of modern research suggests that the upheavals of 1640 onwards were essentially political rather than social. The traditional ruling class remained very much in control. Whatever their differing views on religion and the constitution, the controlling classes invariably closed ranks in the face of a challenge to their customary authority. The Levellers could make little headway against this.

Furthermore, the Levellers were never numerous enough or, indeed, extreme enough to offer a serious threat. They often blustered, and individuals such as Lilburne were capable of exciting considerable fear, but they were never fully committed to the use of force. Even had they been, there was the awesome figure of Cromwell confronting them. As long as the great body of the army remained loyal to their commanders, there was never a realistic chance that the Levellers could impose themselves by force of arms. As Austin Woolrych put it: 'The Levellers were in fact a precociously well-organized pressure group rather than a revolutionary movement, and much more interested in principles than in power'.[3]

It should be noted that the word 'Leveller' was in many ways misleading. Indeed, much of the pamphlet literature that the movement produced was concerned with denying that it intended the levelling of society. Most modern historians now warn against viewing the Levellers as democrats in anything approaching a modern sense. They did not believe in universal suffrage. They wanted the vote for the 'middling sort', by which they meant self-made people as craftsmen, shopkeepers and the smaller property-owners. Their movement never represented the poor and showed no interest in the agricultural labourers. It was almost exclusively an urban movement. In demanding an extended franchise, it deliberately excluded wage earners and servants. As a result, the Leveller movement fell between two stools. It frightened the propertied classes and so was never able to win support among people of influence. At the same time, it failed to appeal to more than a limited section of the lower orders and so never became a broad-based movement.

d) The True Levellers (the Diggers)

> **KEY ISSUE** In what sense were the Diggers true levellers?

The once widely-held view that radicalism was a major force in England at this time has largely been abandoned by modern analysts. There was never a single radical movement. There were various radical groups but these did not come together to form a serious social or political force. They are interesting as forerunners of the liberals and socialists of a later age, but in their own time they did not even remotely suggest that they were capable of taking power – even had that been their aim. Their influence was minimal.

How far the Levellers were from being a truly revolutionary force is evident from a comparison of them with a movement that made a brief and notorious appearance in 1649. Early in that year, a group of about fifty people, calling themselves the 'True Levellers', took over a patch of wasteland on St. George's Hill in Surrey, which they began to cultivate. This was the practical expression of their belief that land and property belonged not to individuals but to the community. They called for an end of private property. In an exact sense, they were communists. Their inspiration was in large part biblical, but they also looked back to a time before the Norman Conquest when, in their belief, Englishmen had been free because the land had been held in common.

Such a movement was too visionary for its time. Harmless though it now appears, it was regarded at the time as an intolerable affront to the established rights of property. The inevitable reaction occurred. The Council of State ordered Fairfax to interrogate Gerard Winstanley and William Everard, the two leading 'diggers', as they were mockingly called. An army unit then supervised the destruction by a local mob of the crops sown on the wasteland. The diggers attempted to carry on with their plan of making 'the earth a common treasury', but local hostility and interference proved too much and the movement collapsed. A similar fate befell the digger colonies that had been set up in ten other southern and midlands counties. At no point did active diggers number more than a few hundred.

4 The Rump and Ireland

> **KEY ISSUES** What was Cromwell aiming to achieve by his campaigns in Ireland?
> Why have his campaigns there traditionally received such a bad press?

When the English Commonwealth was established in 1649, its most immediate task was to subdue rebellion in Ireland and Scotland. Active opposition to the imposition of English authority had been continuous in Scotland since 1637, and in Ireland since 1641. In 1649, having suppressed the royalists in England, the new regime now had the opportunity to crush resistance in the other two kingdoms.

a) The Background to the Irish Crisis

Ireland was the more immediately pressing of the two problems. Following the execution of Charles I, the Stuarts' chief Irish supporter, the Earl of Ormonde, had been successful in persuading the Protestant royalists in southern Ireland to join with the Catholics in a league against Parliament. Charles II, as he had entitled himself immediately on hearing of his father's death, hoped to use Ireland as a base for winning back the Stuart throne. He judged, not unrealistically, that the great mass of the Irish Catholic population had reason to dread the new English Commonwealth. In 1641 the Irish Catholics had risen in an attack upon the Protestant settlers in Ulster. It was an outburst of pent-up rage at the policy of 'plantation' pursued by English governments since Tudor times. Plantation involved dispossessing the native Irish of their land and resettling it with English and Scottish settlers, usually of the most extreme Protestant kind. What had deepened bitterness still further had been the severely repressive religious and financial policies imposed on the Irish Catholics by Strafford as Lord Lieutenant of Ireland in the late 1630s.

Although the Irish rising of 1641 was a bloody affair, it was never as barbarous as the subsequent accounts by English Protestants made out. Nevertheless, it was seized upon by the more extreme Puritans in England as sure proof of the irreversibly evil character of Irish Popery. The English Parliament pledged itself to destroy the Irish 'Antichrist', a term denoting particular detestation for people whose loathsome behaviour was evidence that they belonged to the damned. The attitude derived from a belief in predestination, one of the fundamental Calvinist doctrines of the more extreme Puritans. Strict predestinarians held that human beings fell into one of two groups; the godly, those whom the Almighty had preordained for eternal salvation, and the ungodly, those whom He had preordained for eternal damnation.

Those English parliamentarians who had such beliefs were easily convinced that Charles I's granting of concessions to the Irish Catholics in 1643, a move intended to win them over to his side in the war against Parliament, was part of a grand Popish design to subvert the Protestant religion throughout the three kingdoms. In 1643 Nehemiah Wallington, a Puritan leather-worker, had expressed the attitude of his co-religionists when he had declared: 'surely the Lord will not suffer the king nor his posterity to reign but the Lord at last will require blood at their hands'. Wallington likened Charles I to the biblical King Josiah whose idolatries had led to the Babylonian captivity of the Israelites. It was such reasoning that strengthened Parliament's resolve both to defeat the King and to punish the Irish. The pre-occupation with the civil wars in England delayed Parliament from carrying out this latter pledge, but in 1649 the moment was opportune. From the beginning, therefore, Parliament's campaign in Ireland was more than simply a matter of subduing royalist rebels. It was an occasion for wreaking vengeance on an ungodly people.

b) Cromwell in Ireland

In March 1649, Parliament appointed Oliver Cromwell Lord Lieutenant and commissioned him to put down the Irish rising. After some months' delay, caused by the need to collect adequate supplies, Cromwell landed south of Dublin with 12,000 men early in August. In an odd way, the delay had worked to his advantage since it had encouraged Ormonde to risk an open attack on the English troops already in Ireland. Ormonde had underestimated the strength of the English force and in an engagement at Rathmines early in August his followers had been surprisingly defeated. The effect of this reverse had been to put Ormonde and the royalists on the defensive and to hand Cromwell the initiative even before he arrived in Ireland.

As a consequence, Cromwell's nine-month campaign in Ireland was essentially a matter of advances and sieges of defended positions. Although Ormonde's forces out-numbered the English army, they

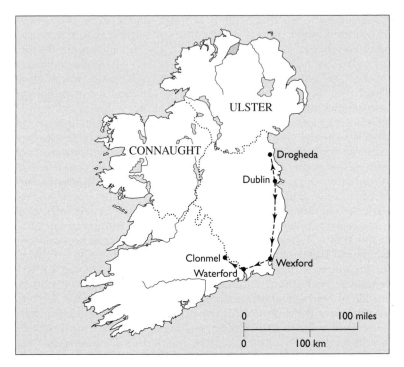

Ireland in the 1650s

were no match for it in artillery or discipline. In addition, Parliament's control of the Irish Sea meant that Cromwell's army was kept regularly supplied, a luxury which Ormonde's troops never enjoyed. It had been Ormonde's hope that Owen Roe O'Neill, the charismatic leader of the Irish peasantry, would bring his forces down from the north to form a royalist combination against Cromwell. However, O'Neill's slowness to respond and then his death in November put an end to such plans. It was, nonetheless, the fear that an alliance between Ormonde and O'Neill might be formed that had led Cromwell to begin his campaign with an advance on Drogheda, a town to the north of Dublin that commanded the main north-south route. The inhabitants put up a stout resistance before the town was taken in a welter of blood. The fall of Drogheda effectively secured the English army's control of the north of Ireland. With this achieved, Cromwell turned back south and began a long advance that within six months brought the whole of the country under his army's domination. It was during the southern march that the town of Wexford was captured, again after a ferocious struggle to overcome the occupants.

The sieges of Drogheda and Wexford have become part of Irish folklore. They are still depicted by some nationalists as typifying the essential brutality of England's approach to Ireland. It is certainly the case that there was a chilling similarity about the fate that befell both places. Each was a fortified stronghold in which civilians had gathered as well as troops. Since the towns were judged to be strategically important, military considerations required that they both be taken. The occupants were first offered quarter if they surrendered. They refused. Cromwell thereupon, in accordance with the rules of war of the time, instructed his troops that once they had stormed the town they were to kill those who had resisted.

As with most atrocity stories, it is difficult to arrive at the exact truth of what then followed. There are modern scholars who suggest that the massacres were not on so large a scale as has been customarily believed. Tom Reilly, an Irish historian, has found no hard evidence that there were any civilian casualties at all at Drogheda. His research further shows that Cromwell at no time during his Irish campaigns ever ordered an attack upon unarmed civilians.[4] Cromwell was careful to limit his blood-letting to those who fought against his forces. He constantly repeated in his various addresses that it was only those who took up arms who need fear his army's wrath. In a Declaration of March 1650, written in response to a protest from a body of Catholic bishops and priests, he claimed that it was the Catholic clergy who had enslaved the minds of the ordinary Irish. His army's aim, he asserted, was to bring liberty to 'a Deluded and Seduced People'.

> 1 We come (by the assistance of God) to hold forth and maintain the lustre and glory of English liberty in a nation where we have an undoubted right to it; – wherein the people of Ireland (if they listen not to such seducers as you are) may equally participate in all benefits, to
> 5 use liberty and fortune equally with Englishmen if they keep out of arms.[5]

Cromwell maintained that his quarrel was not with the Irish people but with their religious and political leaders who had betrayed them into opposing lawful authority.

> As for the people, what thoughts they have in matters of religion in
> 7 their own breasts I cannot reach; but think it is my duty if they walk honestly and peaceably not to cause them in the least to suffer for the
> 9 same, but shall endeavour to walk patiently and in love towards them.[6]

However Cromwell's motives are judged, it remains undeniable that the engagements at Drogheda and Wexford were horrific affairs. In his lengthy reports to Parliament, Cromwell described how desperate the fighting had been on both sides. Detailing the storming of Drogheda, he wrote:

> 1 The enemy retreated, divers of them, into the Mill-Mount, a place very strong and of difficult access ... Our men getting up to them were

ordered by me to put them all to the sword. And indeed, being in the
heat of action, I forbade them to spare any that were in arms in the
5 town ... About one hundred of them possessed St. Peter's church-
steeple ... These being summoned to yield to mercy, refused, where-
upon I ordered the steeple of St. Peter's Church to be fired, where one
of them was heard to say in the midst of the flames: 'God damn me,
God confound me; I burn, I burn' ... When they submitted, their offi-
10 cers were knocked on the head and every tenth man of the soldiers
killed, and the rest shipped for the Barbadoes. I am persuaded that this
is a righteous judgement of God upon these barbarous wretches, who
have imbrued their hands in so much innocent blood; and that it will
tend to prevent the effusion of blood for the future, which are the sat-
15 isfactory grounds to such actions, which otherwise cannot but work
remorse and regret.[7]

Wexford was a repeat of the horrors of Drogheda, with even greater
casualties. In his account to Parliament, Cromwell gave the death toll
as 2,000 and admitted that he and his soldiers had been 'crazed' by
the excitement of battle. He again ascribed the massacre to the will of
God: it was His fitting punishment on the 'Anti-Christ', Cromwell's
term for those ungodly Papists who had been in arms against the
English Protestants since 1641.

His righteous justice brought a just judgement upon them, causing them
to become a prey to the soldier, who in their piracies had made preys
of so many families, and made with their bloods to answer the cruelties
which they had exercised upon the lives of divers poor Protestants.[8]

What should be emphasised is that the grim reputation attaching to
Cromwell in Ireland did not derive from what the Irish said about him
at the time. Many Irish peasants were impressed by Cromwell's
humane treatment of the unarmed civilians caught up in the fighting.
The fearsome image of Cromwell in Ireland was largely a product of
Irish nationalist writers of the nineteenth century and twentieth century who chose to depict him as the personification of English
tyranny. It is an interesting example of history being pressed and dis-
torted to serve a particular cause.

One of the most persistent myths about Cromwell was that he went
to Ireland intent on creating a reign of terror over the Irish people.
This has been shown to be quite contrary to the evidence.
Interestingly it is southern Irish historians who have been foremost in
re-evaluating Cromwell in this regard. Writers such as Tom Reilly and
Jason McElligott have stressed that, from the time he landed in
Ireland to the time he left nine months later, Cromwell insisted that
the persons and property of civilians be fully respected.[9] On first arriv-
ing in Ireland he issued this stern order to his troops:

1 Whereas I am informed that upon the marching out of the armies
heretofore, or of parties from Garrisons, a liberty hath been taken by

the Soldiery to abuse rob, and pillage, and too often to execute cruelties upon the Country people: being resolved, by the grace of God, dili-
5 gently and strictly to restrain such wickedness for the future. I do
hereby warn and require all Officers, Soldiers and others under my
command, henceforth to forebear all such evil practices as aforesaid:
and not to do any wrong or violence toward Country People, or persons whatsoever, unless they be actually in arms or office with the
10 enemy, and not to meddle with the goods of such, without special
order.

And hereof I require all Soldiers, and others under my command,
diligently to take notice and observe the same: as they shall answer to
the contrary at their utmost perils. Strictly charging and commanding all
15 Officers and others, in their several places, carefully to see to it that no
wrong or violence be done to any such persons as aforesaid, contrary
to the effect of the premises. Being resolved, through the grace of God
to punish all that shall offend hereunto, very severely, according to the
Law or Articles of War, to displace and punish, all such Officers as shall
20 be found negligent in their places, and not see the due observance
hereof, or not punish the offenders under their respective commands.[10]

These were not mere words. Cromwell was quick to punish any of his
troops who disobeyed these orders. In his dealings with the Irish
people, he was tough and resolute but he was not gratuitously cruel
or vindictive. It is true that in the heat of battle his measured instructions may have been ignored. Excesses undoubtedly occurred but
they were not part of a deliberate policy. Cromwell kept within the
rules of warfare as they were practised at that time. It was commonly
accepted that if the armed inhabitants of a besieged town were
offered the opportunity to surrender but refused, they thereby for-
feited their right to be treated mercifully should they be defeated .

In his letters from Ireland, Cromwell repeatedly claimed that,
despite their apparent severity, his methods were intended to prevent
a greater 'effusion of blood'. Historians are divided over this claim.
To cite two modern authorities by way of example: Ronald Hutton has
accepted Cromwell's contention that his harsh measures did cow the
Irish into a quicker submission, thereby shortening the struggle and
saving lives. Hutton has further suggested that, judged by the
European standards of his day, Cromwell was not notably severe; he
takes a similar view to Tom Reilly and argues with reference to Ireland
that 'to magnify the actions of Cromwell remains a glaring example
of bad history'.[11] A different emphasis has been given by Barry
Coward, a major biographer of Cromwell. He has pointed out that the
Drogheda and Wexford massacres did not terrorise the other garrisons into rapid surrender, and that the towns of Dungarvan,
Waterford and Clonmel fell to Cromwell only after determined and
prolonged resistance. In taking Clonmel in April 1650, the English
army suffered the loss of over 2,000 men.[12]

Whatever difficulties Cromwell may have faced, there is no doubt that by the time of his recall to England, in May 1650, his principal aim had been achieved. The royalist cause in Ireland was a lost one. Henry Ireton took over as commander of the English forces, but his task, and that of Charles Fleetwood who succeeded him, was essentially a mopping-up operation. In completing Cromwell's subjugation and settlement of Ireland, Ireton and Fleetwood took decisions of the utmost significance for the future of Anglo-Irish relations. The previous plantation polices were continued. To prevent further Irish risings, the lands of the defeated royalist leaders were confiscated and given to Protestant settlers. Over 40,000 Catholic families were dispossessed. By 1660, Catholic ownership of land was a bare 20 per cent, compared with 60 per cent in 1641. This had the additional effect of further reducing the condition of the mass of the Catholic peasantry, whose only possible future was as despised and ill-protected labourers under the new Protestant landed ascendancy.

This policy was not simply a matter of retribution against the Irish rebels. The expropriation of land provided a way for the Commonwealth to meet some of its heavy financial commitments. Soldiers were encouraged to accept land in Ireland in lieu of their arrears of pay. Land was also offered to the many creditors that Parliament had acquired since 1642. All this suggests that it was finance as much as religious or political principle that dictated the Commonwealth's policy towards Ireland.

5 The Rump and Scotland

> **KEY ISSUE** Why were the Scots unable to mount an effective resistance to the Rump?

a) The Background to the Scottish Crisis

Scottish resistance to the English parliament was a mixture of nationalism and religion. The Scots had long objected to political dictation from London, whether by king or parliament. They especially resented being subject to the Anglican Church with its system of interfering bishops and priests. One of the reasons why Calvinism was so attractive to the Scots was that it proposed the ending of Anglicanism and its replacement by a Scottish Presbyterian state church. The Solemn League and Covenant in 1643 (see page 7) had committed the English Parliament to introducing this. However, developments within Parliament following the defeat of the King in 1646 threatened to destroy Scottish hopes. By the time of the Second Civil War in 1648, Presbyterian influence in the Long Parliament had been superseded by that of the Independents, the representatives of the Protestant congregations, who objected to exchanging one form of state church for another. Frustrated by this turn of events, the Presbyterians began to consider that an alliance with Charles I might now be a better way of achieving their original aims.

Charles sought to take advantage of the divisions in the Protestant ranks. He was quite prepared to compromise his position as head of the Anglican Church by entering into an agreement with the Scottish Covenanters. In December 1647 he signed an 'Engagement' with a Presbyterian faction led by the Duke of Hamilton, in which he undertook to adopt Presbyterianism as the state religion in return for military support to enable him to subdue Parliament.

Despite the defeat of the King in the Second Civil War, the 'Engagers' remained the dominant influence in Scotland at the time of his execution. They immediately proclaimed his son as their lawful monarch, Charles II. The new King hoped that this would lead to a full-scale Scottish uprising on his behalf, but the division within Scotland between Presbyterians, Episcopalians and Catholics prevented a united front from being formed. This was illustrated by the failure of the Earl of Montrose, the Stuarts' most dedicated supporter in Scotland, to mount a serious royalist challenge to the Rump. Nonetheless, Charles persevered. In April 1650 he declared his willingness to enter into agreement with the Scots. Two months later, he returned in person to Scotland and formally swore to the Covenant on terms very similar to those his father had accepted in 1647. Charles II's willingness to take the Covenant and form an alliance with the Marquess of Argyll, the leading Covenanter, had been quickened by the execution of Montrose in May 1650 at the hands of the Rump's representatives in Edinburgh.

b) Cromwell in Scotland

It was the growing Scottish danger that obliged the Rump to recall Cromwell from Ireland in 1650. When Fairfax declined to lead the English army against the Scots, Cromwell was appointed in June to replace him as Lord General and Commander-in-Chief. Cromwell declared that he felt no personal animosity towards the majority of the Scots, whom he regarded as his Protestant brothers. He appealed to them to consider 'in the bowels of Christ' whether they were not grossly mistaken in opposing the English Parliament. Even after setting out on his march north, Cromwell continued to issue conciliatory addresses to the Scots; he spoke of his 'longing to have avoided blood in this business'. It has been suggested that this explains the relative uncertainty of his military judgements during the Scottish campaign. In August he was frequently outmanoeuvred by David Leslie, the commander of the Covenanter forces. But whatever Cromwell's minor tactical errors may have been, when the two armies did finally meet at Dunbar, early in September, he was incisiveness itself.

Cromwell's defeat of the Covenanters at the battle of Dunbar is widely regarded by military historians as his greatest success as a soldier. Despite his army's being outnumbered by two to one and initially having been in a potentially disastrous position, his judgement, coolness under fire, and power to inspire his troops, produced an overwhelming victory. The Covenanters were left broken and dispirited; many of them interpreted their defeat as a sign of God's anger at their having dared to fight on Charles II's side. Dunbar did not mark the end of the Scottish campaign. Cromwell remained in Scotland until well into 1651, but then, as he had in Ireland, he left subordinate generals to complete the subjugation. John Lambert and George Monck carried out the task ruthlessly and successfully.

Yet Charles II did not allow the crushing of the Covenanters to destroy his own hopes. In a bold attempt to achieve in England what he failed to do in Scotland, he marched south into England with a force of 12,000. His hope was that his personal presence would inspire a royalist uprising. It was not to be. The response was small-scale and disorganised, and it was a despondent royalist army that finally confronted Cromwell's forces at Worcester on 3 September 1651, the anniversary of Dunbar. This time the strategic position was reversed; Cromwell had by far the larger army. He used the superiority in numbers to rout the royalists. Charles accepted defeat and after eluding near capture fled abroad into an exile that was to last nine years.

The Rump proceeded to declare that Scotland was now totally under its authority. The Edinburgh parliament was dissolved and the power of the Presbyterian church was greatly reduced; it was ordered to tolerate the existence of the individual protestant sects in Scotland. In addition, the Scottish people were required to pay for the upkeep of the English army of occupation. It was the Rump's belief that these measures would extinguish for good the embers of royalism in Scotland.

6 The Record of the Rump

> **KEY ISSUE** How successful was the Rump in the years 1649–53?

Until relatively recently, the Rump Parliament had a very poor reputation. It tended to be regarded as an incompetent oligarchy, which clung to power for four years until it was forcibly dissolved by an exasperated Oliver Cromwell in April 1653. However, modern researches, most prominently those of David Underdown and Blair Worden, have led to an adjustment of this dismissive view of the Rump.[13] What now tends to be emphasised is the severity of the problems that preoccupied the Rump.

a) Religious Policy

The civil wars had left the position and character of the Established Church very uncertain. In 1645, Parliament had recommended the adoption of Presbyterianism, but had made no real effort to implement this. The Rump was divided on the issue. The Presbyterians, with their desire for a centrally-controlled state church, were roughly equal in number to the Independents, who stood for the principle of permitting the local congregations (sometimes referred to as 'the gathered churches') to pursue their own form of worship. So evenly split was the Rump that it required the casting vote of the Speaker to defeat a proposal in August 1649 that Presbyterianism should be confirmed as the state religion of England. In addition to the two main groups, there were a number of MPs who cannot be easily labelled, except by such confusing terms as 'independent Presbyterians', who favoured some form of compromise such as maintaining a central church while denying it a controlling authority over the local congregations. This was a notion with which Oliver Cromwell sympathised (see page 75).

What is clear is that, whatever the differences of opinion within the Rump over the formal structure of the Church, few MPs wished society to be left completely free in matters of morality. The majority of members were more concerned to take the opportunity provided by the new Commonwealth to impose 'godliness' (a code of moral conduct) upon the nation than to allow liberty of conscience. Acts were introduced that imposed penalties for adultery, fornication and profane language. 'An Act against Blasphemy' was passed in 1650 with the aim of curbing the more extreme sectarians, such as the Ranters who claimed that since they belonged to the ranks of the godly they could do no wrong and therefore were not subject to the law (see page 72). The absence of more sweeping measures indicated that the Rump had no real intention of reforming the Church along the lines hoped for by the religious radicals. It was not until late in 1650, and then with some reluctance, that the Rump finally repealed the statutes passed in Elizabeth's reign that had required Sunday worship in the Anglican church. On the vexed questions of tithes (taxes levied for the upkeep of the clergy), the Rump did nothing; the clergy continued to be paid in the old way.

Since the days of Archbishop Laud, it had been very clear that control of the pulpit was the key factor in deciding what form of worship was followed in the localities. The appointment of the clergy was, therefore, of vital concern and the Rump frequently discussed how this could best be organised. However, precisely because it was such a sensitive question, no clear decision was reached. It is true that 'A Committee for the Propagation of the Gospel' was appointed by the Rump in 1652, with the intention of creating a system for the strict supervision of clerical appointments. But the wide divisions within

Parliament over religion meant that there was no final agreement over the standards by which the suitability of individual clerics was to be judged.

There is no doubt that in the country at large the shock of the King's defeat and execution had encouraged the growth of millenarianism, the belief that the momentous events of the day were a sign that a great cataclysm, such as the second coming of Christ, was imminent. Some believed that since the end of the world was nigh, the old forms of church and government no longer mattered and, therefore, should be abandoned (see page 69). As a body, the Rump was far from representing this attitude. In matters of religion, as in politics, its basic conservatism meant that it resisted radical calls for a complete break with the past. To limit the flood of millenarian broadsheets and pamphlets that appeared in London and elsewhere, the Rump imposed press censorship. In a further effort to counter criticism, it published its own government journal, *Mercurius Politicus*, which presented an official version of public affairs.

b) Legal and Social Policies

Demands for reform of the law were heard from sectarians, Levellers and the army. These interest groups were divided in what they wanted from reform, but they agreed that the existing legal system had to be changed. The main objections to the current legal practice were that it was the preserve of the privileged, prohibitively expensive, and scandalously slow in operation. The lawyers themselves were widely despised as corrupt manipulators. The law as it stood was seen by many as an expression of the 'Norman yoke' that had oppressed Englishmen and denied them their freedom since the days of William the Conqueror almost 600 years previously. Reformers called upon the Rump to curb the power of the lawyers and open the law to all by simplifying its complex procedures. The Rump certainly gave thought to legal reform. Among its positive steps were the adoption of more lenient methods for punishing debtors and the authorisation of the use of English in the courts instead of Latin and French. But it did nothing to ensure lower legal fees or to provide easier access to the courts for the ordinary person.

The Rump's reluctance to consider major changes in the law is largely explained by the composition of the Commons. Of the 211 MPs who attended the House during the Commonwealth period, nearly 50 were from the legal profession. The largest single group among the average of 60–70 members who attended the daily sessions of Parliament was composed of lawyers. Such men were naturally reluctant to undertake changes that would weaken their privileged position.

The same was true of another interest group which was strongly represented in the Commons, the merchant traders. They used their influence to prevent interference with current commercial practices, such as monopolies, and were instrumental in the Rump's passing of the Navigation Act of 1651 (see page 88). What was true of the legal and commercial interests applied to the Rump overall. It contained few dedicated republicans intent on sweeping change. Its primary aim was to gain the support of the established classes in society. A policy of moderation and regard for existing structures was far more likely to win over men of influence and authority in the localities. It was the provincial gentry, the traditional ruling order, whom the Rump were trying to impress.

The Rump did give some attention to proposals for social reform, which included schemes for the extension of education and for some form of poor relief. How genuine their interest was in this area cannot be easily assessed since in practice the demands of war and the maintenance of national security deprived them of both the time and the resources to turn such proposals into reality. Such pressures gave the Rump limited opportunity to engage in reform.

An interesting aspect of the period is that the day-to-day operation of the law in the communities continued largely unchanged. This was a testimony to the underlying strength and stability of local institutions, and a reminder that the decisions of central government did not always determine what actually happened at local level.

c) Financial Policies

Judged by the amount of revenue it gathered, the Rump was a highly successful body. It raised finance through taxation, assessment (taxes on land), excise levies, and the sale of Crown lands and church property. These were supplemented by the proceeds of confiscated royalist estates. However, this last policy, while being a useful source of revenue, proved politically short-sighted since it made it difficult for royalists to reconcile themselves to the Commonwealth. Confiscation also contravened the spirit of the Pardon and Oblivion Act, which had been passed in 1652 with the intention of winning over those who had previously supported Charles I.

In spite of its successful financial policies, the Rump still remained short of money. Its revenue could not keep up with the cost of the campaigns in Ireland and Scotland and of the war against the Dutch (see pages 88–89). It is important to stress again that the Rump had to spend so much time and revenue in running the various wars in which it became engaged that it was restricted in what it could do on the domestic front. The Rump cannot be said to have failed through want of trying. If anything, it tried too hard. As its legislative record indicates, there were clear signs that its energies had begun to flag by 1653. For four years it had been in almost constant session, sitting four or five days a week throughout the year.

Much of the Rump's work was done through committees.

The Rump Parliament in action

Total number of MPs who attended the House between 1649–53:
211

Active members: 60–70

Average attendance: 50–60

Number of Legislative Committees Established
152 in 1649   98 in 1650   61 in 1651   51 in 1652   12 in 1653

Number of Acts passed
125 in 1649   78 in 1650   54 in 1651   44 in 1652   10 in 1653

% of legislation devoted to particular issues
security and finance – 51%
local government and the army – 30%
social problems – 9%
economic and social reform – 4%
religion – 3%
law reform – 3%

However, there was no precise pattern of business, and co-ordination between the various committees was often poor. A further complication was that the boundaries of authority between the Council of State and the Commons were blurred, a situation which was partly explained by the fact that the Council was largely made up of sitting MPs.

Yet, it was not so much the administrative problems of the Commonwealth that weakened it, as the assumption by the sectarians and the republicans that the Rump was merely a stage on the road to either the rule of the saints or the establishment of a full-blown republic. In view of the pressures on it from outside, its own internal divisions, and the military burdens it carried, the Rump's achievement of four and a half years of stable government was remarkable. Nor must it be forgotten that the Rump's subjugation of Ireland and Scotland ranks as an extraordinary feat by any measure.

7 The Dissolution of the Rump, April 1653

> **KEY ISSUE** What factors explain the dissolution of the Rump in 1653?

The Rump was never expected to be a permanent body. Indeed, in September 1651 it had made provision for its own dissolution, by

voting to disband itself by the end of 1654. It had also set up a committee to supervise the drafting of plans for a 'new representative'
parliament. However, this failed to impress the Army Council, which
considered that the Rump had subsequently amended the rules governing parliamentary elections so as to ensure that the existing members would retain their seats. The notion that the Rump was
manoeuvring to prevent a genuinely new parliament from being elected offended the two main groups who had become increasingly dis-
illusioned with the Commonwealth – the republications, whose main
spokesman was Colonel John Lambert, and the Fifth Monarchists (see
page 71), whose leader was Colonel Thomas Harrison. Both men had
personal reasons for disliking the Rump since each felt he had been
slighted by being denied promotions within the regime's gift.

However, in the event, it was Oliver Cromwell who forcibly ended
the life of the Rump. Considerable research has been conducted into
his motives. Not all historians who have studied the question are in
agreement. Nevertheless, the broad lines of the story can be established. What appears to have happened is that in April 1653 the
Rump, rather than carry on indefinitely, had actually begun to consider a bill that would have brought forward its dissolution by over a
year. However, the army's fear was that this was simply a ruse to disguise the fact that the qualifications being written into the bill would
result in any new parliament being composed of substantially the
same members.

How well-founded the army's suspicions were is impossible to
judge since the only copy of the bill was torn up by Cromwell at the
time he dissolved the Rump. His anger seems to have been aroused
not so much by the bill itself but by the Rump's going back on a promise they had previously given him that they would suspend their consideration of it. On 20 April he marched to Westminster at the head
of a column of troopers, entered the Commons, and told the startled
members that their sitting was at an end and that they must leave.
'You have sat here too long for the good you do. In the name of God,
go!'. After a token protest by a few MPs, they did as they were told.
The next day a wag nailed to the door of the Commons a notice that
read: 'This House is to be let, now unfurnished'.

Cromwell's role was obviously the critical one in the ending of the
rule of the Rump, but it is important not to anticipate events by
assuming that his eventual move had always been part of his plans.
For the whole of the period 1649–53, he had remained the servant of
Parliament, a position which he loyally accepted, as shown by the letters and reports that throughout the Irish and Scottish campaigns he
faithfully sent to the Speaker. Moreover, the evidence suggests that,
despite the firmness with which he acted in April 1653, he had genuinely agonised over the decision to use force to end the Rump. It is
true that after Pride's Purge in 1648 the Rump depended on the
goodwill of the army, but it would be wrong to think of the military as

a constant threat to Parliament. Indeed, although the army often urged MPs to pursue certain courses of action, it rarely tried to impose its will directly upon the Commons.

A striking example of this, was Parliament's consistent refusal to accept the army's *Heads of Proposals*, first drawn up in 1647, as a basis for constitutional reform. The Proposals, which included a programme of parliamentary and legal reforms, as well as plans for the final settlement of the arrears owed to the army, were still being pressed upon the Rump as late as 1652. John Kenyon suggests that this 'astonishing demonstration of the army's impotence' is an important corrective to the notion of the Rump's existing for four years under the shadow of the military.[14] One reason for the army's restraint was its pre-occupation between 1649 and 1652 with the Scottish and Irish wars. Another is the attitude of its Commander-in-Chief. Right up to the time he dissolved the Rump, Cromwell appears to have wanted it to succeed. His religious ideas may have been radical, but his social and political views were conservative. As his later rule as Protector was to show, he never lost his belief in Parliament as an essential part of any constitutional settlement. He held his army in check until he became outraged by the Rump's failure to live up to his expectations of it.

References

1 David Underdown, *Pride's Purge: Politics in the Puritan Revolution*, OUP, 1971, p. 262.
2 Ivan Roots (Ed.), *Speeches of Oliver Cromwell*, J.M. Dent, 1987, p. x.
3 Austin Woolrych, *England Without a King*, Methuen, 1983, p. 15.
4 Tom Reilly, *Cromwell, An Honourable Enemy*, Phoenix Press, 1999, pp. 4, 116.
5 W.C. Abbott (Ed.), *The Writings and Speeches of Oliver Cromwell*, Cambridge, Mass, 1937–47, vol. II, p. 205.
6 *Ibid*, p. 203.
7 *Ibid*, p. 127.
8 *Ibid*, p. 142.
9 Tom Reilly, *Cromwell, An Honourable Enemy*, Phoenix Press, 1999, Jason McElligott, *Cromwell, Our Chief of Enemies*, Dundalgan Press, 1994.
10 W.C. Abbott (Ed.), *The Writings and Speeches of Oliver Cromwell*, Cambridge, Mass, 1937–47, vol. II, pp. 111–12.
11 Ronald Hutton, *The British Republic, 1649–60*, (Macmillan, 1990, p. 48.
12 Barry Coward, *Oliver Cromwell*, Longman, 1991, p. 75.
13 David Underdown, *Pride's Purge: Politics in the Puritan Revolution*, Oxford, 1971, Blair Worden, *The Rump Parliament*, CUP, 1974.
14 John Kenyon, *The Stuart Constitution*, CUP, second edition, 1986, p. 298.

Working on Chapter 2

Even a cursory reading of this chapter will indicate that a great deal happened in the years 1649 to 1653. It is important not to get lost in detail; the sub-sections into which the chapter is divided offer a convenient way of concentrating on essential developments. There are a number of key aspects of the story to grasp. These are:

1. the Rump's relations with the army,
2. the Leveller challenge,
3. the Cromwellian subjugation of Ireland and Scotland,
4. the dissolution of the Rump in 1653
5. the record of the Rump.

Use the Key Issues and the Summary diagram to help you plot your course through the chapter.

Answering structured and essay questions on Chapter 2

The following questions relate to the separate sections in this chapter. The questions are closely linked to the Key Issues that are there to guide you through the material you are reading. These will point you to the information and ideas that you need. You will notice that some questions are straightforward in that they ask you to *describe*, while others are more demanding in that they ask you to *explain*. In the first case you have simply to use your *knowledge* to answer the question; in

Summary Diagram
The Rump Parliament, 1649–53

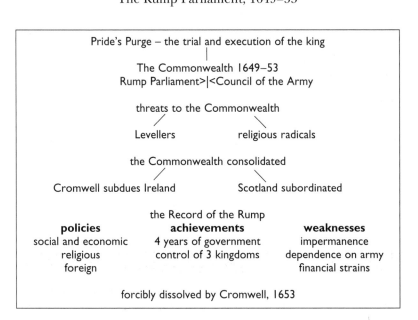

the second case you have to use your *judgement*. Put simply, it is the difference between being asked *what* happened and being asked *why* it happened.

No matter what type of question you are attempting, it is always worth your drawing up lists of key facts and points. If you find that the question is the straightforward descriptive type, then a well-ordered and shaped list will provide the plan for your answer. If, however, you are being asked for an explanation or a judgement, then your list will provide the backing evidence that you then use in developing your argument.

I. a) Describe the main ways in which Pride's Purge altered the composition and structure of Parliament.
   b) How far do you agree with the view that 'in effect, Pride's Purge left England under military rule'?
2. a) Trace the main steps by which the Rump overcame the challenge from the Levellers.
   b) Was it the weakness of the Levellers or the strength of the Rump that led to the failure of the Leveller movement in the early 1650s? Give reasons in support of your answer.
3. a) Describe the chief features of Cromwell's military campaign in Ireland, 1649–50.
   b) 'When set against the military conventions of his time, the remarkable thing about Cromwell's Irish campaign is how restrained it was.' How acceptable do you consider this view to be?
   c) Explain why neither the Irish nor the Scots were able to achieve a successful rising against the Rump.
4. a) In what ways did the Rump attempt to solve the religious and financial problems that it faced?
   b) Examine the view that 'the Rump does not deserve the bad press it has customarily received'.
5. a) Trace the main events that led to the dissolution of the Rump in April 1653.
   b) How did Cromwell justify his forcible dissolution of the Rump in April 1653? How convincing do you consider his justifications to have been?

Source-based questions on Chapter 2

1 Cromwell and the Levellers
Study the extracts from Oliver Cromwell's statement on page 22. Answer the following questions:

a) Explain the meaning of the following terms, as used by Cromwell: 'the guilt and blood and treasure shed and spent in this kingdom' (page 22 lines 2–3). (*5 marks*)
'a despicable, contemptible generation of men' (lines 7–8). (*5 marks*)
b) Using your own knowledge, examine the ways in which Cromwell

fulfilled his own assertion that 'you have no other way to deal with these men but to break them' (lines 1–2). (*10 marks*)

c) Assess the strength and weaknesses of this source as evidence of Cromwell's attitude towards the Levellers. (*15 marks*)

2 *Cromwell in Ireland*

Study the extracts from Cromwell's reports on pages 31–32, from his Declaration on page 31, and his instructions to his army on pages 32–33. Answer the following questions:

a) Put into your own words what Cromwell meant by the following:
   i) 'it is my duty if they walk honestly and peaceably not to cause them in the least to suffer' (page 31, lines 7–8) (*5 marks*)
   ii) 'it will tend to prevent the effusion of blood for the future' (page 32, lines 13–14). (*5 marks*)

b) In his reports, on page 32, how does Cromwell justify his army's actions during the sieges of Drogheda and Wexford? (*8 marks*)

c) Using your own knowledge and the evidence in the sources, say how far you agree with the suggestion that Cromwell was 'remarkably restrained in his dealings with Ireland during the years 1649–50'. (*15 marks*)

e) In what ways are these sources valuable to the historian as evidence of English attitudes towards Ireland in this period? (*15 marks*)

3 The Search for a Settlement, 1653–8

POINTS TO CONSIDER

Between 1653 and 1658 England experimented with various forms of government in a series of attempts to establish a stable constitution. This chapter examines each of those experiments in turn: the Nominated Assembly 1653, the First Protectorate Parliament 1654–5, the rule of the Major-Generals 1655–7, and the Second Protectorate Parliament 1657–8. The dominant figure in all this was Oliver Cromwell. It was he who initiated the experiments and it was his hopes and frustrations that were the main factors in determining the unfolding of events. Your chief aim, therefore, should be to follow his moves as described in the various sub-sections. The chapter also frequently refers to the controversies that surround the question of what motivated Cromwell. Make sure that you also grasp the main points of these.

KEY DATES

1653	**April**	Rump Parliament and Council of State dispersed.
	Jul–Dec	Nominated Assembly gathered.
	July	New Council of State appointed by the Assembly.
	Dec	Nominated Assembly dissolved itself.
		Instrument of Government adopted.
		Cromwell became Lord Protector.
1654	**April**	Act of Union with Scotland.
	Sept	First Parliament of the Protectorate.
1655	**Jan**	Cromwell dissolved first Protectorate Parliament.
	Mar	Penruddock's rising.
	Oct	Beginning of the rule of the Major-Generals.
1656	**Sept**	Second Protectorate Parliament.
		Parliament's prosecution of James Nayler.
1657	**Jan**	Parliament declined to renew Decimation Tax.
		Rule of Major-Generals ended.
	Feb	Cromwell offered the kingship.
	Apr	Cromwell declined the kingship.
	May	Cromwell accepted *Humble Petition and Advice*.
	July	First session of Parliament.
1658	**Jan–Feb**	Second session of Parliament.
	Feb	Cromwell dissolved Parliament.
	Sept	Death of Oliver Cromwell.
		Richard Cromwell became Protector.

1 The Nominated Assembly, July–December 1653

> **KEY ISSUES** What did Oliver hope to achieve by convening the Nominated Assembly?
> Why was the Assembly so short-lived?

Cromwell's forcible dissolution of the Rump and the Council of State left the Commonwealth under direct military rule. Yet, although the Army Council now held power, they immediately took steps to try to restore constitutional forms. On behalf of the Army Council, Cromwell announced that a new assembly was to be established, not by election but by nomination. After his officers had vetted lists of reliable persons in the localities, he issued the following summons to 140 selected individuals:

1 Forasmuch as, upon the dissolution of the late Parliament, it became necessary that the peace, safety, and good government of this Commonwealth should be provided for; and in order thereunto, divers persons fearing God and of approved integrity and honesty are, by
5 myself, with the advice of my Council of Officers, nominated; to whom the great charge and trust of so weighty affairs is to be committed; and having good assurance of your love to, and courage for, God and the interest of his cause and of the good people of the Commonwealth; I, Oliver Cromwell, Captain General and Commander-in-Chief of all the
10 armies and forces raised and to be raised within this Commonwealth, do hereby summon you … to be and appear at the Council Chamber at Whitehall upon the 4th day of July next, then and there to take upon you the said trust; unto which you are hereby called and appointed.[1]

Cromwell's summons to 'persons fearing God' led to the Assembly's being referred to as the 'Parliament of the Saints'. Alternative names by which it became known include: the 'Nominated Assembly', the 'Little Parliament' and 'Barebone's Parliament'. This last title came from the attempt by royalists and republicans to ridicule the Assembly, whose legitimacy they refused to accept, by naming it after one of its back bench members, Praise-God Barebone, a London leather-seller.

As the wording of the summons shows, the Nominated Assembly represented Cromwell's attempt to achieve stable rule in England by entrusting government to the godly. This used to be interpreted by historians as a concession to the ideas of Harrison and the Fifth Monarchists (see page 71), who had urged that a ruling body like the sanhedrin (council) of the ancient Israelites should be established. However, modern writers have seen it more as a compromise between the ideas of Harrison and those of John Lambert, the leading republican, who had wanted government to be carried on, in the interim before a full republic could be established, by a council nominated by the army. In its final form, the 140-member Assembly was exactly twice the size of the sanhedrin model, which enabled it to appear more representative than a smaller body would have been.

As with the Rump earlier, the Assembly was not intended to be permanent. This is clear from its decision to fix a date, November 1654, for its own dissolution. At the time of its first meeting in July, the Assembly appointed a new Council of State of 31 members. This contained a number of officers, including Cromwell, but the majority were civilians. Soon after it first gathered, the Assembly declared itself to be a parliament. This did not please Cromwell and was the first sign that the Assembly would disappoint his expectations.

By selecting men of 'approved integrity', the Army Council had hoped that the Assembly would prove amenable and responsible. But, from the beginning, there was a sizeable minority of members who refused to be overawed by the military. These were largely Fifth Monarchists and the extreme sectarians who genuinely believed that Christ's Second Coming was imminent. To prepare for this, they demanded the sweeping away of all forms of organised religion and the abolition of all existing law. This was a rejection of the social order and the rights of property. Although the fanatics were a minority, their extremism overshadowed proceedings and tended to be taken as characteristic of the Assembly as a whole during its five-month existence. The moderates and conservative members eventually grew exasperated with the extremists and concluded that the only way to stop them was to dissolve the Assembly. Accordingly, in December, the moderates met in a special session, from which the wildest of the sectarians were excluded, and voted to end the parliament. In doing this, they gave back to Cromwell the authority he had granted them.

The tame ending of the Nominated Assembly should not be taken to mean that it had been a total failure. It is true that it disappointed the hopes of reformers. Cromwell later referred to his calling of the Nominated Assembly as 'a story of my own weakness and folly' and admitted that 'these 140 honest men could not govern'. But scholars now recognise that the work of the Assembly marked a key period in the development of public administration in England. Among the proposals which it discussed in the 15 committees into which it divided were the reform of the law on debt, humane treatment of the insane, the civil registration of births, deaths and marriages, and greater protection for travellers on the highways. In many respects these measures were ahead of their time. After the Restoration it became customary to dismiss this Assembly as if it had been composed simply of inexperienced social upstarts. This was a false picture. Austin Woolrych has made a detailed study of the Nominated Assembly's composition;[2] among his important findings are the following:

- 116 of the members ranked as gentry (substantial landowners)
- 119 members were JPs in their local communities
- 40 members had attended university, while another 40 had trained as lawyers
- 24 members had sat in a previous parliament, and 67 would be elected to later parliaments
- Nearly all the members had experience of administration

There are good grounds, therefore, for speculating that had the Nominated Assembly not been riven by the religious issue it would have performed as effectively as any of the other parliaments of the period. Like them, it was weakened by its failure to reconcile social conservatism and religious fanaticism.

2 The Founding of the Protectorate

> **KEY ISSUE** What powers did *the Instrument of Government* grant to Cromwell as Protector?

Cromwell claimed to have known 'not one tittle' about the manoeuvre by which the moderates had outwitted the extremists and ended the life of the Nominated Assembly. Yet the evidence suggests that he had already lost faith in it. He had been particularly annoyed by its proposal to end the monthly assessment (property tax), a move which he interpreted as an attack upon the military, since it was the assessment which paid for the upkeep of the army. What is certain is that he was fully aware of the *Instrument of Government*, the alternative constitution that had been drawn up even before the Assembly dissolved itself. This was the work of John Lambert, one of the brightest of the younger officers, who for some time had been pressing for a written constitution that would give the republic stability.

The *Instrument* provided for a Lord Protector, who was to hold governmental powers and be aided by a Council of State, and a single-chamber parliament of 400 members from England and Wales which was to meet at least once every three years for a minimum of three months. In addition, Ireland and Scotland were to be represented in the House by 30 MPs apiece, thus making it the first-ever truly British parliament. In a direct repudiation of Leveller ideas, the *Instrument* stipulated that the franchise was to be restricted to men of substance. The possession of property or income of a value of at least £200 was made the basic qualification for voting. Papists and known royalists were debarred from voting or standing for election. In an attempt to settle the religious question, the *Instrument* declared somewhat imprecisely that there was to be a national church professing 'sound doctrine'. Liberty of worship was to be the right of 'such as profess faith in God by Jesus Christ', with the exception of papists and those guilty of 'licentiousness', a reference to the extreme sectarians. The *Instrument* also declared that there was to be a standing (permanent) army of 30,000 soldiers.

The speed and smoothness with which the *Instrument* was adopted indicates that Cromwell was well prepared for it. In November he had held discussions with Lambert and the army officers, and had keenly supported the drafting of a new constitution, provided it did not involve his being made 'King Oliver'. Cromwell's objection was meant to scotch rumours that had been circulating for some months that he contemplated being made emperor or king. Cromwell preferred the renewal of the title of 'Lord Protector' since this office had a number of precedents in English history going back to the fifteenth century. It was his way of maintaining links with the ancient constitution, while at the same time distancing himself from the recently disgraced and overthrown monarchy.

Within four days of the ending of the Nominated Assembly, the *Instrument* had come into force and Cromwell had been installed as Lord Protector. During the following nine months, before the meeting of the first parliament of the Protectorate in September 1654, Cromwell worked with the Council of State in drafting a large number of ordinances which he intended to present to Parliament for ratification. The measures covered a wide range. They included financial reform and the regularising of the two main types of taxation in operation, the 'assessment', which was a monthly locally-raised tax on property, and the 'excise', a centrally-imposed tax on goods and commodities.

Other ordinances of importance were those concerned with religious reorganisation (see page 75) and those carrying forward the legal and administrative reforms, first suggested but not implemented under the Rump. Cromwell regarded sound laws as essential to the well-being of the nation and recognised that it was their unjust application that caused most laws to be unpopular. He told his second Protectorate Parliament:

1 There is one general Grievance in the Nation. It is the Law ... and the great grievance lies in the execution and administration ... To hang a man for sixpence, thirteen pence, I know not what; to hang for a trifle, and pardon murder – is the ministration of the Law, through the ill-
5 framing of it.[3]

While there was no doubting that the Protectorate had now become the effective constitution, its legitimacy remained in question throughout its six-year existence (1653–9). The *Instrument of Government* from which the Protectorate derived its authority was solely the product of the Council of Officers; it never received full civilian backing and was never formally ratified by any of the parliaments called during these years. It was a governmental system imposed by the military, something which Cromwell remained very conscious of throughout his time as Lord Protector. This is worth stressing, for it corrects the notion that the Protectorate parliaments were merely obstructive bodies standing in the way of reform and progress. The MPs who challenged the *Instrument* and Cromwell's authority under it had as much or as little right to do so as the Army Council had in imposing it originally. After all, Parliament could claim that it was an elected body, whereas the Army Council represented nobody but themselves.

3 The First Protectorate Parliament, September 1654–January 1655

> **KEY ISSUE** What strains developed between Cromwell and his first parliament?

Under the terms of the *Instrument*, a parliament was scheduled to meet in September 1654. The elections for it took place during the preceding summer months. The army did not interfere with the elections, which Gerald Aylmer judges to have been 'as free as any in the seventeenth century'.[4] Certainly the results did not return a House submissive to Cromwell and the army. The 460 members included Presbyterians, republicans, and even some royalist sympathisers. The decision, taken in accordance with the *Instrument*, to transfer seats to the more populous counties at the expense of the corrupt borough constituencies had the important effect of increasing the number of independent country-gentry members.

Cromwell had hoped that the new Parliament would quickly implement the ordinances he and the Council of State had drafted. He was to be disappointed. Although in his opening address he reminded the assembled MPs that their first duty was to provide the people of England with 'good and wholesome laws', the new parliament gave priority not to reform but to an attack on the *Instrument*. The republican MPs (known as Commonwealthsmen), who claimed that Cromwell's dissolution of the Rump had been unlawful, led the assault. They challenged the right of the Protector to exercise the civil and military authority granted him by the *Instrument*, and criticised the composition of the Council of State, complaining that it contained too many army officers. They also objected to the high cost of maintaining the standing army that had been sanctioned by the *Instrument*. They demanded that it be reduced from 50,000 to 30,000, as laid down in the new constitution.

It has been Cromwell's declared wish that this Parliament would begin 'healing and settling' the religious differences that divided the nation. However, far from taking a conciliatory line, Parliament voiced its concern at the tolerance that had already been shown under the Protectorate. Cromwell tried to lessen the growing opposition by obliging the MPs to take an oath of loyalty to the Protectorate. This resulted in the exclusion of 100 members who refused to swear allegiance, but it did not greatly diminish the criticism of his regime. None of the 84 ordinances which Cromwell had previously prepared was passed by Parliament. Nor was Parliament content simply to obstruct his proposals. It sought to restrict his powers as Protector by introducing a new constitutional bill which would have effectively undermined the authority granted him under the *Instrument*. This proved the final straw for Cromwell; in January 1654 he dissolved Parliament after just five months' sitting. When doing so, he defined four 'fundamentals' on which he believed government should rest:

> 1 Government by a Single Person and a Parliament is a fundamental! That Parliaments should not make themselves perpetual is a fundamental. Is not liberty of conscience a fundamental? The army should not have absolute power; neither should that authority which governs the army
> 5 have absolute power – that is a fundamental.[5]

4 The Major-Generals, 1655–7

> **KEY ISSUES** What powers did the Major-Generals have?
> How successful was the rule of the Major-Generals?

1655 was a critical year for the Protectorate. In addition to the failure of Parliament to fulfil Cromwell's hopes, royalist and republican opposition threatened in the country at large (see pages 77–78). Rumours of Leveller or republican plots to assassinate the Lord Protector circulated widely. These dangers encouraged Cromwell to look to his natural allies, the army commanders, as a way of ensuring not simply military security, but administrative efficiency as well. This led to the introduction of a system of direct military government, known as the rule of the Major-Generals. The decision to adopt this experiment was not Cromwell's alone; it was taken after lengthy consultation with the Army Council. John Lambert, who was himself to be one of the Major-Generals, was a leading proponent of the scheme. In the late summer of 1655, England was divided into 11 (subsequently 12) districts responsible not only for exercising military control but also for overseeing the operation of local government.

In their official Instructions the Major-Generals were granted unprecedentedly wide powers and duties:

> 1 They are to endeavour the suppressing [of] all tumults, insurrections, rebellions or other unlawful assemblies which shall be within the said counties respectively ...
> 2 They are to take care and give order, that all papists and others who
> 5 have been in arms against the parliament, or assisted the late king or his

---

The Major-Generals and the Counties they Controlled

John Barkstead – Middlesex
James Berry – Wales and Worcestershire
William Butler – Northants, Huntingdonshire, Bedfordshire
John Desborough – Gloucs, Wiltshire, Dorset, Somerset, Devon, Cornwall
Charles Fleetwood – Norfolk, Suffolk, Essex
William Gough – Berkshire, Hampshire, Sussex
Thomas Kelsey – Surrey and Kent
John Lambert – Yorks, Cumberland, Westmoreland, Northumberland
William Packer – Oxfordshire, Buckinghamshire
Philip Skippon – London
Edward Whalley – Derby, Notts, Lincoln, Warwickshire, Leicestershire
Charles Worsley – Lancashire, Cheshire and Staffordshire

---

son in the late wars, as also all others who are dangerous to the peace
of the nation, be disposed of, as may be for the public service ...
6 They shall in their constant carriage and conversation encourage and
promote godliness and virtue, and discourage and discountenance all
10 profaneness and ungodliness; and shall endeavour with the other justices of the peace, and other ministers and officers who are entrusted
with the care of those things, that the laws against drunkenness, blas-
pheming and taking of the name of God in vain, by swearing and curs-
ing, plays and interludes, and profaning the Lord's Day, and such-like
15 wickedness and abominations, be put in more effectual execution than
they have been hitherto ...
19 All gaming houses and houses of evil fame [brothels] be industriously
sought out and suppressed within the cities of London and
Westminster and all the liberties thereof ...
20 21 All alehouses, taverns and victualling houses towards the outskirts of
the said cities be suppressed, except such as are necessary and convenient to travellers; and that the number of alehouses in all other parts
of the town be abated, and none continued but such as can lodge
strangers and are of good repute.[6]

The most striking aspect of the work of the Major-Generals was the
introduction of the Decimation Tax. This was a 10-per-cent levy
imposed on known royalists with annual incomes of more than £100.
The measure was intended both to prevent further risings, such as
Penruddock's, which occurred in March 1655 (see pages 77–78), and
to provide finance for the Major-Generals, who had authority to raise
local troops in order to maintain the army's strength. It was hoped
that the new tax would thus be the means both of preserving a powerful standing army and avoiding a heavy charge on central government
funds.

Although, for the sake of convenience, historians have tended to
treat the rule of the Major-Generals as if it were a single system, the

type of administration in each of the 12 districts depended very much on how the individual Major-General chose to carry out his instructions. For example, while Whalley, Kelsey and Worsley (who is reputed to have closed down over 200 ale houses) were renowned for their industry and sense of duty, Gough frankly acknowledged that he was not up to the task.

What appears to have made the Major-Generals unpopular was their interference with everyday life in the localities, especially their attempt, in accordance with Instruction 6, to impose moral behaviour upon the inhabitants. Moreover, their military rank could not disguise the fact that they were of a lower social status than the local gentry over whom they had been placed. For magistrates and officials who functioned in what was very much a hierarchical order, the intrusion of social upstarts into the conduct of affairs was particularly distasteful.

An additional irritant was that few of the Major-Generals were local to the area they controlled. This created a strong feeling among the people in the communities that they were now subject to outside rule. One of the features of mid-seventeenth century England on which modern historians are agreed is that local loyalties predominated over national ones. National consciousness did exist, as the popular support for foreign wars often indicated, but people's first thoughts were for their own local concerns. Consequently when intrusive government was imposed from outside, no matter how well-intentioned or efficient it might be, it offended local feelings. It was this that made it so difficult for the rule of the Major-Generals to gain acceptance. The problems that this created for Cromwell illustrate how far he was from exercising total power as Protector. His authority was considerable but it was never absolute. Barry Coward has observed:

1 The contribution of Cromwell and the Council [of State] to the stability and efficiency of the government of England in the 1650s is, of course, limited. Their personal intervention in favour of 'healing and settling' and reform were spasmodic and did not amount to a co-ordi-
5 nated 'policy' of centralisation; nor did they have the bureaucratic machinery to carry one out.[7]

The same limitation applied to the Major-Generals. The strictness of their rule and the resentment it aroused have been customarily taken as proof of their effectiveness as centralising administrators. Derek Hirst, another authority on the period, has challenged this interpretation. He has written that 'the assumption that the major-generals represent the high point of early-modern centralisation is open to question ... historians have been misled by the intensity of the major-generals' labours'.[8]

The evidence suggests that during the 1650s local institutions continued to function in the traditional way, regardless of the political changes and developments that took place at the centre. Magistrates' courts operated as they had done before the civil wars. In the previous decade, county committees appointed by Parliament had largely replaced the traditional rule of local Justices of the Peace. However, the decision of the Rump to cease funding the county committees had seen their disappearance and the re-emergence of the JPs as the principal local administrators. In any case, Cromwell had no wish to undermine the authority of the leaders in the communities; it would have suited him far better if the Major-Generals could have established harmonious relations with the local gentry. However, if that was the intention, it failed, since the system had begun to founder on the rock of local resistance long before Cromwell had lost faith in it.

Given that Cromwell had at his disposal a large, highly successful and godly army, it made sense for him to use it as an instrument for the creation of a godly nation. He claimed in a speech to Parliament in September 1656 that the Major-Generals had been 'very effectual towards the discountenancing of vice and settling religion, than anything else these fifty years'.[9] This was wishful thinking. Religion had not been settled. Furthermore, the unpopularity that the regime had aroused outweighed whatever individual successes might have been achieved. Although it had not been Cromwell's intention, the rule of the Major-Generals had challenged the independence of the local gentry; it had imposed taxes and raised local militia without parliamentary authority and with little reference to the opinion of the leaders in the community. In the parliamentary elections, held in the summer of 1656, the protest slogan 'no swordsmen, no decimators' was widely voiced, an indication of how unpopular the Major-Generals had become.

As a system of control, the Major-Generals were not part of the *Instrument of Government*. They were intended to fill the gap before the next parliament. They did not, therefore, take Cromwell any nearer to solving the problem of how to achieve stable, non-military rule. Indeed, it seemed even clearer that stability and order depended wholly on his military authority.

5 The Second Protectorate Parliament, 1656–8

> **KEY ISSUE** How significant were the 'new' Cromwellians?

a) The First Session, September 1656–July 1657

The decision to summon a new parliament, a year earlier than was required under the *Instrument*, was prompted by the need to raise money. As with the Stuarts before him, Cromwell found it difficult to run the government on the income he was granted by his various parliaments. It was not that he was unduly extravagant. Although his wife and daughters lived in some style, Cromwell's Protectorate 'court' at

Whitehall was certainly not lavish by royal standards. He himself lived relatively frugally.

Nonetheless, the administrative and military costs of the Protectorate were high. A parliamentary report in 1655 revealed that the government's annual revenue, made up from such sources as customs and excise, assessments and fines on royalists, amounted to £2,250,000, whereas military, naval and civil expenditure was £2,611,532. The deficit was increased by the added military costs occasioned by the war against Spain that began in 1656 (see pages 90–92). It was the necessity of raising extra finance that led the Major-Generals to advise Cromwell to call another parliament. They told him that they would be able to monitor the elections so as to ensure that only co-operative members would be returned.

It was certainly true that greater efforts were made to shape the composition of the House than at the time of the first Protectorate Parliament. When the new Parliament met in September 1656, 100 members were declared ineligible and prevented from taking their seats. The early signs were that this purge had produced the desired result, since the first months of the session were relatively quiet. Cromwell congratulated the members on their ready attention to business and their willingness to provide money for the Spanish war.

However, it was not long before friction occurred. The first major difficulty arose over the House's prosecution for blasphemy of the Quaker, James Nayler. This was a matter in which Parliament, in Cromwell's judgement, had exceeded its powers (see pages 73–74). It was against this background of strained relations between Protector and Parliament that the second crisis of the session occurred. In January 1657, John Desborough, the main spokesman for the Major-Generals, introduced a bill to renew the decimation tax for the maintenance of the militia in the counties. Since the upkeep of the Major-Generals depended upon this tax, to vote against the bill was to vote against their regime. This is precisely what Parliament proceeded to do. The defeat of Desborough's militia bill marked the effective end of the Major-Generals as a system of government. Cromwell's reaction was angry, but his anger was directed as much against the Major-Generals for advising him to call Parliament in the first place as against the MPs who had opposed the bill. He did not formally abandon the system of Major-Generals; it was simply allowed to lapse.

That Cromwell did nothing to save the system pointed to the ambiguous position in which he now found himself. Support for him at this point in his Protectorship came from two main sources. One obvious group was the army leaders, such as the Major-Generals, who saw him as their representative, someone concerned to use military strength as the guarantee of national security and strong government. Their experience ever since the civil wars had made them suspicious of all parliaments, which they regarded as self-seeking oligarchies rather than as guardians of liberty and the constitution.

Cromwell as Lord Protector
The ceremony which accompanied his installation lent credence to the idea
that he was king in all but name. Cromwell, however, was not carried away
by it all. When the size of the crowd lining the streets of the procession was
pointed out to him, he remarked, 'There would have been an even greater
throng to see me hanged.'

The second group has been identified by modern historians, most notably by Austin Woolrych, as the 'new Cromwellians'.[10] The term refers to those in public life who wished to see the Protectorate become an essentially civilian government. The group included important military figures, such as General Monck, Cromwell's commander in Scotland, and Lord Broghill, a one-time royalist but now a staunch friend and confidant of the Protector. However, it was largely composed of civilian politicians; leading lawyers such as Bulstrode Whitelocke and William Lenthall were prominent among them. These men were traditionalists in that they believed in the virtues of the old constitution and the social order, but they were sufficiently flexible to accept that the Protectorate could be reshaped so as to incorporate the social and political values that they prized. They held that the more Cromwell was able to distance himself from the military, the closer he would move towards making the Protectorate an acceptable and permanent system of government. By allowing the rule of the Major-Generals to fall into disuse, Cromwell was responding to the wishes of the 'new' Cromwellians.

b) The Humble Petition and Advice, 1657

> **KEY ISSUE** Why did Cromwell decline the offer of kingship?

The new Cromwellians formalised their views in a document which eventually became known as the *Humble Petition and Advice*. This was an alternative written constitution to the *Instrument of Government* and was offered to Cromwell in March 1657. It proposed that Cromwell should become king, be granted adequate financial resources, and rule with a restored Privy Council and with regular parliaments that would include an upper house. This renewal of kingship was meant not to extend Cromwell's authority but to limit it. What was envisaged was not the absolute monarchy which the Stuarts had tried to exercise before 1640, but a constitutional monarchy in which parliament would be an equal and permanent partner.

One aspect of the *Humble Petition and Advice* certainly attracted Cromwell. Since the offer of the new constitution had come from Parliament, it would have a validity and legality that the *Instrument*, the creation of the Army Council, had lacked. He certainly gave the offer much thought. This is evident from a number of contemporary accounts. As early as 1652, Cromwell, in a conversation recorded by Bulstrode Whitelocke, had spoken of the attractions of monarchy:

1 And surely the power of a king is so great and high and so universally understood and reverenced by the people of this nation that the title of it might not only indemnify in a great measure those that act under it, but likewise be of great use and advantage in such times as these, to
5 curb the insolences and extravagances of those whom the present powers cannot control.[11]

During the spring of 1657, rumours that Cromwell was seriously considering becoming king led to a series of petitions from the army officers urging him to reject such a course. They appealed to him to remain faithful to 'the good old cause'. After weeks of discussion and soul-searching, which he described as causing him great 'consternation of spirit', Cromwell finally informed Parliament in April that he had decided not to accept the title of king. He offered the following reason:

> 1 It was said that kingship is not a title, but an office, so interwoven with
> the fundamental laws of the nation that they cannot, or cannot well, be
> executed and exercised without it – I cannot take upon me to repel
> these grounds; for they are strong and rational. But if I shall be able to
> 5 make any answer to them, I must not grant that they are necessarily
> conclusive: ... Truly the providences of God hath laid aside this title of
> king providentially and this not by sudden humour or passion; but it
> hath been by issue of as great deliberation as ever was in a nation. It
> hath been the issue of ten or twelve years civil war wherein much blood
> 10 hath been shed ... I will not seek to set up that that Providence hath
> destroyed and laid in the dust.[12]

In the end, therefore, Cromwell had chosen to stay loyal to what the army leaders called 'the good old cause'. Despite this, some sections of the army still remained uneasy about his intentions. Part of the problem was the long delay between the offer of the crown and his refusal of it. In Maurice Ashley's words, Cromwell's decision 'alienated his new friends while his prolonged hesitations displeased his old ones'.[13]

Cromwell's rejection of kingship was not a rejection of the proposed new constitution itself. In May he duly accepted the *Humble Petition* in a modified form. He was to remain 'His Highness, the Lord Protector Oliver' and was empowered to name his successor and to appoint the members of the 'Other' (upper) House. For some, this was kingship in all but name. Edmund Ludlow, an ardent republican and representative of those Commonwealthsmen who had been suspicious of Cromwell's aims ever since his dissolution of the Rump in 1653, regarded the revised version of the *Humble Petition* as merely the climax of a Cromwellian plot to extend the Protector's powers still further.

This now seems a harsh verdict. Cromwell's acceptance of the new constitution suggests his anxiety to arrive at a settlement that would unite the whole nation. It is striking how often the word 'settlement' figured in his letters and speeches around this time. For example, addressing a parliamentary committee in April 1657, he said:

> 1 You have need to look at settlement. I would rather I were in my grave
> than hinder you on anything that may be for settlement, for the nation
> needs it and never needed it more ... I am hugely taken with the word
> Settlement, with the thing and with the notion of it. I think he is not
> 5 worthy to live in England that is not ... A nation is like a house, it cannot
> stand without settlement.[14]

Cromwell's position as Protector under the new constitution of 1657 represented a compromise. He had strengthened the civilian base of the Protectorate, but the army still remained the major force within it. This was clear in the way Cromwell used his authority as Protector to appoint a large number of his officer colleagues to seats in the Other House. Since this upper chamber of 40 members had the right to veto legislation of which it disapproved, it possessed considerable constitutional power. Republications were swift to condemn an arrangement which subordinated the will of Parliament to the whim of the army. They complained that the *Humble Petition and Advice* was no more than a tinkering with the existing system. It left Cromwell and the army in control.

At the end of July 1657, a month after Cromwell's second formal installation as Protector, Parliament went into recess. Already there were signs that the adoption of the *Humble Petition* had not solved Cromwell's problems. He was obliged to dismiss from the Privy Council John Lambert, his long-standing colleague and the creator of the *Instrument of Government*, for refusing to take the oath of loyalty to the new constitution. It may well be Lambert acted out of career intentions, hoping that by detaching himself from involvement in the new constitutional arrangements he would be in a strong position should they prove unworkable. But whatever Lambert's personal motives, the incident indicated that Cromwell had failed in his aim of establishing a government sufficiently representative to be widely acceptable.

c) The Second Session of Parliament, January–February 1658

The House of Commons that reassembled in January 1658 was significantly different from the one that had gone into recess six months earlier. The members who had been excluded at the beginning of the first session in September 1656 now returned. These were largely republicans. They had been debarred originally on the grounds that they were 'unfit' persons as defined by the *Instrument of Government*. But, now that a new constitution had been adopted, that technicality could no longer be invoked by the government to keep them out. Their return was an important victory for the republicans. Led by Arthur Haselrig, who believed that all government had been illegitimate since the dissolution of the Rump, they launched into an attack on the new constitution. Among their targets were the authority of the Protector, the power of the army, high taxation, and foreign policy.

Cromwell's difficulties were increased by the depletion of his supporters in the lower house, the most able of whom he had transferred to the Other House. Fearing that the parliamentary onslaught might lead to his political and religious enemies combining, he decided to end the sitting. His particular reason for dissolving Parliament after a session of less than a month was to prevent it from considering a republication petition that called for the abandonment of the Protectorate and the restoration of the Rump. Cromwell's deepest worry was that the petition was rumoured to have found favour with some of the troops.

Cromwell's letter dismissing John Lambert

OLIVER CROMWELL AND THE INTERREGNUM

-Profile-

1649	signed Charles I's death warrant
	crushed the Levellers
1649–50	campaigned in Ireland
1650–51	campaigned in Scotland
1653	forcibly dissolved the Rump
	became Lord Protector
	convened the Nominated Assembly
1654	called First Protectorate Parliament
1655	dissolved First Protectorate Parliament
	established rule of the Major-Generals
1656	called Second Protectorate Parliament
1657	abandoned rule of the Major-Generals
	declined to become king
1658	dissolved Second Protectorate Parliament
	died
1660	body disinterred and publicly hanged

In 1658, at the time of the dissolution of what proved to be his last parliament, Cromwell had scarcely seven months to live. In traditional descriptions he is often portrayed in this period as an ageing man, weakened by illness, and in despair at his failure to achieve a settlement. The picture is exaggerated. While it is true that on occasion he was incapacitated by the malaria which he had contracted during his Irish campaigns, he remained highly active until at least the last month of his life. He supervised the workings of day-to-day government and paid particular attention to foreign policy. He had certainly not given up all hope of a settlement in England. His frequent discussions with the army officers and his readiness where necessary to dismiss those of doubtful loyalty showed his determination to preserve army unity and with it the nation's security. His greatest problems remained financial. The annual income of £1,300,000 that he had been granted under the *Humble Petition* fell short of his governmental costs by £500,000. As had Charles I before him, he found it increasingly difficult to raise loans from the City. This was no doubt why he drew up plans for the calling of another parliament later in the year.

When Cromwell became Protector in 1653 he had faced a number of demanding questions. How was a stable executive government to be created to replace traditional monarchy? What was to be the place of Parliament? Was the army to continue to play a political role? How was government to be effectively financed? How were the religious differences in the nation to be settled? At his death on 3 September 1658, these issues remained largely unresolved. Some sceptics have suggested that it was never his intention to resolve them, that his essential aim was to wield power, not to reach settlements. Many contemporaries held that view and it has been restated periodically ever since. However, most modern historians incline to the view that to regard Cromwell simply as a military leader exercising authority for its own sake is to disregard the strength of his religious and political motivation. Even though he did not achieve his aim, there is no reason to doubt the sincerity of his desire to reach a just and godly settlement.

> Everybody doth nowadays reflect upon Oliver and commend him, so brave things he did and made the neighbour princes fear him.
>
> *(Samuel Pepys, Diaries, 1667)*

> As he had all the wickedness against which damnation is denounced, and for which hell-fire is prepared, so he had some virtues which have caused the memory of some men in all ages to be celebrated; and he will be looked upon by posterity as a brave bad man.
>
> *(Clarendon, The History of the Rebellion and Civil Wars, 1702)*

> Cromwell is scarce ever mentioned but with detestation, or thought of but as a monster.
>
> *(Cato's Letters, 1721)*

> No sovereign ever carried to the throne so large a portion of the best qualities of the middling orders, so strong a sympathy with the feelings and interests of the people.
>
> *(Thomas Carlyle, On Heroes and Hero Worship, 1841)*

> A better Christian, a more noble-minded spirit, a greater warrior, a more constant man has scarcely ever appeared on the face of the earth.
>
> *(a resolution of the Wallington Mutual Improvement Society, 1852)*

> He sought to justify himself and the Revolution he led by appeals to a glorious future. It was this that made him so preoccupied with ends and not with means, and this in turn justified his disregard for civil rights whenever anyone or anything stood in the way of what he took to be God's purpose.
>
> *(John Morrill, Revolution and Restoration, 1992)*

References

1 S.R. Gardiner (Ed.), *The Constitutional Documents of the Puritan Revolution 1625–1660*, OUP, 1906, p. 405.
2 Austin Woolrych, *Commonwealth to Protectorate*, OUP, 1982.
3 R.C. Richardson & G.M. Ridden (Eds.), *Freedom and the English Revolution*, Manchester UP, 1986, p. 39.
4 Gerald Aylmer, *Rebellion or Revolution*, OUP, 1986, p. 169.
5 Ivan Roots (Ed.), *Speeches of Oliver Cromwell*, J.M. Dent, 1987, p. 51.
6 John Kenyon, *The Stuart Constitution*, CUP, second edition 1986, pp. 322–24.
7 Barry Coward, *Oliver Cromwell*, Longman, 1991, p. 167.
8 Derek Hirst, *Authority and Conflict: England, 1603–1658*, Edward Arnold, 1986, p. 338.
9 W.C. Abbott (Ed.), *The Writings and Speeches of Oliver Cromwell*, Cambridge, Mass, 1937–47, vol. IV, p. 274.
10 Austin Woolrych, *England Without a King*, Methuen, 1983, p. 34.
11 Ivan Roots (Ed.), *Speeches of Oliver Cromwell*, J.M. Dent, 1987, p. 211.
12 W.C. Abbott (Ed.), *The Writings and Speeches of Oliver Cromwell*, Cambridge, Mass, 1937–47, vol. IV, pp. 467–73.
13 Maurice Ashley, *England in the Seventeenth Century*, Penguin, 1954.
14 W.C. Abbott (Ed.), *The Writings and Speeches of Oliver Cromwell*, Cambridge, Mass, 1937–47, vol. IV, p. 484.

Working on Chapter 3

By using the Key Issues boxes and the *Summary* diagram, you will be able to gain a clear idea of the efforts made to produce a lasting political settlement in this period. Take each of these attempts in turn (Nominated Assembly 1653, First Protectorate Parliament 1654–5, Major-Generals 1655–7, Second Protectorate Parliament 1657–8) and break them down into manageable and memorable sections by asking yourself three questions about each of them – a) What were the aims behind it? b) What were its main features? c) How far did it achieve its aims? Cromwell was, of course, the central figure in all this. To gain an appreciation of his position and attitude, pay close attention to the two written constitutions which he accepted and which defined his authority as Lord Protector – the *Instrument of Government* and the *Humble Petition and Advice*.

Summary Diagram
The Search for a Settlement, 1653–8

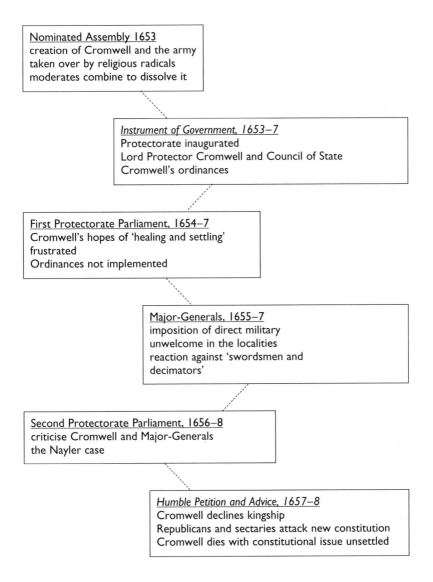

Nominated Assembly 1653
creation of Cromwell and the army
taken over by religious radicals
moderates combine to dissolve it

Instrument of Government, 1653–7
Protectorate inaugurated
Lord Protector Cromwell and Council of State
Cromwell's ordinances

First Protectorate Parliament, 1654–7
Cromwell's hopes of 'healing and settling'
frustrated
Ordinances not implemented

Major-Generals, 1655–7
imposition of direct military
unwelcome in the localities
reaction against 'swordsmen and
decimators'

Second Protectorate Parliament, 1656–8
criticise Cromwell and Major-Generals
the Nayler case

Humble Petition and Advice, 1657–8
Cromwell declines kingship
Republicans and sectaries attack new constitution
Cromwell dies with constitutional issue unsettled

Source-based questions on Chapter 3

1 The Cromwellian Principles of Government

Study the '4 fundamentals' on page 52 and Cromwell's observations on the law on page 50, and then answer the following questions:

a) According to the '4 fundamentals', what does Cromwell regard as the basic constitutional requirements in the English state? (*5 marks*)

b) As described by Cromwell in the extract on page 50, what were the prevailing weaknesses in the legal system? (*5 marks*)

c) How useful to a historian are these two extracts as illustrations of the governmental problems that faced Oliver Cromwell as Protector? (*15 marks*)

2 The Rule of the Saints and of the Major-Generals

Study the summons on page 47, the Instructions on pages 52–53, and the comment by Barry Coward on page 54. Answer the following questions:

a) Using your own knowledge and the evidence in the summons, examine the reasoning behind Cromwell's calling of the Nominated Assembly. (*10 marks*)

b) In what ways does evidence contained in the Instructions explain the subsequent unpopularity of the Major-Generals? (*10 marks*)

c) How far does the evidence in the summons and in the Instructions support Coward's contention as expressed in the extract on page 54? (*15 marks*)

3 Cromwell and Kingship

Read the extracts from Cromwell's conversation on page 58 and Cromwell's address to parliament on page 59.
Answer the following questions:

a) According to the evidence in the extract on page 58, what was Cromwell's attitude towards monarchy as an institution? (*10 marks*)

b) How adequate are these extracts as an explanation of Cromwell's reasons for declining the offer of kingship? (*10 marks*)

c) Using these extracts and your own knowledge, i) describe the circumstances, and, ii) analyse the consequences, of Cromwell's decision not to accept the title of king in 1657. (*15 marks*)

Answering Structured and essay questions on Chapter 3

Structured questions are the type that begin with such leads as 'Describe ...', 'Describe how ...', 'Show how ...', 'In what ways did ...?' and 'Describe the ways in which...' Typical questions based on the material in this chapter might be:

1 In what ways did the Nominated Assembly represent Oliver Cromwell's notion of rule by the godly?
2 Describe the main differences between the *Instrument of Government* and the *Humble Petition and Advice*.
3 What were the main duties and functions of the Major-Generals, 1655–57?
4 Describe the main difficulties that Oliver Cromwell encountered in his dealings with the Second Protectorate Parliament, 1656–58.
5 What political problems were left unresolved at the time of Oliver Cromwell's death in 1658?

Essay questions tend to fall into one of two categories. One type asks you to explain causation, that is to analyse why things occurred the way they did or asks you to make a judgement on a historical proposition. The questions on causation are usually in a 'why?' form with such leads as, 'Why was ...?', 'Explain why ...' and 'Account for ...'. Examples might be:

6 How would you account for the unpopularity of the rule of the Major-Generals, 1656–57?
7 Why was the Nayler case such an important issue between Oliver Cromwell and the Second Protectorate Parliament?
8 Why, despite its attractions, did Oliver Cromwell decline the offer of kingship in 1657?

Examples of questions calling for your judgement might be:

9 How successful do you consider the Nominated Assembly to have been?
10 How acceptable do you find the suggestion that 'the protectorship of Oliver Cromwell created more problems than it solved'?

Consider question 9. You are being asked to make a judgement. It would not be adequate for you simply to describe the work the Assembly did and the problems it faced. Your task is to estimate its degree of success. When tackling any question that involves an assessment of success or failure, it is very helpful to set down what the original aims of the individual were. If you do that, you are then in a position to say how far the aims were achieved. This is an effective way of evaluating success. In this instance, state what Cromwell's hopes were for the Assembly. Did his hopes coincide with the aims of the members? Does the fact that the Assembly dissolved itself mean that Cromwell's experiment had necessarily failed?

Challenges to the Protectorate – the Sectaries and the Royalists

4

POINTS TO CONSIDER

This Chapter builds upon the study of the Protectorate made in the previous chapter. Here the emphasis shifts from the constitutional developments and the difficulties that Cromwell had with the republicans to the religious and political threats to his Protectorate that came from the sectaries (religious radicals) and the royalists. The greater part of Cromwell's domestic policies was concerned with meeting the challenge offered by those who, for religious or political reasons, refused to accept his rule. This chapter analyses the pressures and tensions which gave shape to the politics of the time and provides an assessment of Cromwell as Protector. As you read the chapter try to form your own opinion about Cromwell's main strengths and weaknesses as a politician.

KEY DATES

1650s   Growth of the major sects, including the Quakers.
1651   Charles II fled abroad after his defeat at Worcester.
              Beginning of the Fifth Monarchy movement.
1653   'The Parliament of the Saints'.
              Ordinances setting up 'Triers and Ejectors'.
1655   Penruddock's Rising in Wiltshire in 1655.
1656   The James Nayler case.
1657   Cromwell rejected the offer of the Crown.

1 The Radical Sectaries

> **KEY ISSUE**   Why was religion such a demanding issue during the Interregnum?

Judged by the amount of attention paid to it, the most pressing concern of the day was religion. It was the great issue that defied settlement. What made it so was the religious splintering that had followed in the wake of the civil wars. The challenge to the established Anglican Church and the ending of censorship in the

1640s encouraged the growth of separatist denominations which rejected the idea of a central state church. Ten years had seen a great change. In 1640 there had been two main Protestant Churches: in England, the Anglican with its Arminian and Puritan wings; in Scotland, the Presbyterian with its strongly Calvinist beliefs. In contrast, by the early 1650s, there were scores of separatist sects in existence, none of them willing to conform to the dictates of an established church, Anglican or Presbyterian.

In order to understand why the sects flourished we need to set them in the context of their time. The upheavals of the 1640s, climaxing with the abolition of monarchy, had created a ferment of ideas, and had convinced many that they were living in a unique period. This conviction was expressed in the 1650s in a widespread belief in 'providence', the concept that events are never random and isolated but are part of a larger divine plan. Cromwell himself had declared: 'The Lord hath done things amongst us as have not been known these thousand years'. For the radical sectaries it was a short step from a belief in providence to an utter conviction that the extraordinary events which had occurred were portents of some great cataclysm. This thought-process is often described as 'millenarianism'. Strictly, the word refers to a particular belief in the imminence of the millennium, the thousand-year period during which Jesus Christ would return to reclaim the earth and govern it with his saints. However, the term is often extended to include all those who believed that a great and revolutionary change in the order of things was about to take place in England.

The extreme forms of millenarianism were deeply disturbing to the civil authorities. It is not difficult to understand why. Those who believed that the end of the world was at hand were very ready to dispense with existing laws and practices. The wilder millenarians asked why they should bother with man-made laws and regulations when God himself was about to sweep all such things away.

Since the sectaries played such a prominent role during the Interregnum, it is necessary to understand the beliefs of the main sects that came into being or into prominence during the English Revolution: the Baptists, the Congregationalists, the Fifth Monarchists, the Muggletonians, the Quakers, the Seekers and Ranters, and the Shakers. The numbers belonging to each sect are difficult to assess, but they cannot have been large. For example, the Baptist movement in the 1650s represented barely one in 400 of the population. However, it was not their numbers that gave the sects significance, but their disruptive ideas. It was these that frightened the authorities into believing that they were faced by forces intent on destroying existing society.

In defining sectarian ideas we should be careful not to give them more precision than they actually had. Many of the sectaries were inspired as much by emotional impulse as by rational theology. That is why they were so impatient with the traditional type of church organisation and worship which had been based on prescribed doctrine. It also explains why many of them did not restrict themselves exclusively to membership of one sect. For instance, Laurence Clarkson, who ended up as a Muggletonian, had begun his religious life as an Anglican; in between, he had been variously a Presbyterian, an Independent, a Particular Baptist, a Ranter and a Seeker.

a) Baptists

The Baptist movement, which had begun earlier in the century, became particularly prominent during the 1640s. Its central belief was that faith was a matter of personal experience and acceptance; it could not be taught or learned. Infant baptism was, therefore, meaningless. Great importance was placed upon the act of adult baptism, usually by total immersion in water, as an expression of the individual's choosing to become one with Christ. Such a practice and belief involved a direct denial of an organised church led by priests or ministers with authority to teach and to administer sacraments.

The movement became divided between 'General' Baptists, those who were willing to co-operate with other sects, and 'Particular' Baptists, those who believed in remaining exclusive. In the 1650s, the Baptists became detested by religious and political conservatives. This was because the movement was thought to be associated with the Anabaptists of sixteenth-century Munster, a group who had been notorious for their defiance of the law and social convention. In truth, there was little connection between the English and German forms apart from the similarity of name, but in the religious controversies of the mid-seventeenth century such distinctions easily became blurred. Baptists tended to look to Cromwell to protect them, and he certainly did intervene on a number of occasions to prevent their persecution by parliament.

b) Congregationalists (Independents)

It would be misleading to think of congregationalism as a particular denomination. The term refers broadly to the separatist or independent Protestant congregations who rejected the idea of a national centrally-administered church. It is often used to describe the 'gathered churches', those congregations of godly persons who came together to worship in the spirit of the Lord. This activity often covered a wide range of viewpoints. Since congregationalism did not seek to impose a rigid theology, many former Anglican priests found themselves able to make the transition into congregational pastors.

That Oliver Cromwell was regarded as an Independent is instructive. He was not opposed to church organisation as such but he believed it must be a voluntary association; it ought not to be imposed on believers. In this respect, Cromwell may be viewed as an interesting representative of congregationalism, one of the more moderate religious movements of is time. On a number of occasions, when the extreme sectaries threatened to create religious chaos, the Congregationalists closed ranks with the Presbyterians and Anglicans.

c) Fifth Monarchists

The clearest expression of millenarianism was to be found among the Fifth Monarchists. This sect, which never numbered above 10,000, drew the majority of its members from the army and included officers, chaplains and troopers. Colonel Thomas Harrison became their leading spokesman. They derived their central belief from the book of Revelations in the New Testament and the book of Daniel in the Old. They interpreted these as prophesying that five great monarchies would rule the earth in sequence. They believed that the Assyrian, the Persian, the Greek and the Roman had been the first four, and that the execution of Charles I had ushered in the fifth and greatest monarchy, the reign of King Jesus. It followed that the government of England must be given over to the rule of the Saints. The Fifth Monarchists' great opportunity seemed to have arrived with the convening of the Nominated Assembly in 1653. However, the subsequent failure of the 'Parliament of Saints' left them embittered. They turned their anger against Cromwell whom they had hailed earlier as a second Moses. They remained a constant political irritant throughout the Protectorate, challenging his authority and accusing him of thwarting God's purpose on earth.

The more fanatical among them posed a real threat to Cromwell's life. Fifth Monarchists were to be found behind the majority of assassination attempts against him, the most notorious being the plot organised by Thomas Venner in 1657 to murder Cromwell as a prelude to the enforced establishment of the rule of the Saints in England. Neither the crushing of this rising nor the death of Cromwell marked the end of their efforts. They made further unsuccessful challenges to the government in 1659. Despite the execution of Thomas Harrison as a regicide in 1660, the Fifth Monarchists made one last unavailing attempt under Venner to overthrow the State in 1661.

d) Muggletonians

This sect took its name from Lodowick Muggleton, a London tailor, who believed that Christ had visited him in person and given him the power to save or damn all other men. This was an extension of the predestinarian ideas he had drawn from his earlier Calvinism. The small sect he formed in 1652, made up unsurprisingly of those whom he had declared to be saved, saw no need to seek converts. Assured of their own unique virtue, they felt free to reject any state or church laws that impinged upon them. The Muggletonians were far too small a group to represent a serious challenge to the social or political order. Nevertheless, their extremist views made them useful bogeymen to be used by the authorities as a warning against the dangers of permitting too much religious toleration.

e) Seekers and Ranters

These two groups may be usefully taken together since there was considerable overlap between them. They are both interesting examples of the type of religion that is based upon feelings rather than theology. Their basic conviction was that God manifested Himself not as an external power but as a spiritual force within the individual. Believers should, therefore, 'seek' the divine spirit not in an organised church or even in the Bible but within themselves by responding to their own promptings. The Ranters gained their name from the practice of declaiming their thoughts aloud whenever the inspiration took them. What made such groups dangerous in the eyes of the authorities was their flouting of social convention. Ranters tended to live communally with wives and property held in common, which gave opportunity for opponents to condemn them as sexually depraved. It was largely in order to check the activities of the Seekers and Ranters that the Rump introduced the Blasphemy Act of 1650. The importance of these two sects historically lies in the fact that their idea of an inner light or spirit became the essential tenet of the Quakers, the most politically and socially disturbing of the religious movements of the 1650s.

f) Quakers

KEY ISSUE Why did authorities find the Quakers so troublesome?

The most clearly defined rejection of the authority of church and state was to be found in the Quaker movement which began in the early 1650s under the leadership of George Fox and James Nayler and grew by the end of the decade to be over 50,000 strong. The fundamental Quaker belief was that the Lord's message came to individuals directly through the 'inner light' of their own personal inspiration, 'God within them'. Since there was no intermediary between God and man, only the Lord Himself was entitled to obedience. It followed that all earthly authority, whether political or religious, was a corruption and that all earthly officials were undeserving of respect or obedience. Quakers often expressed their beliefs with a vigorous disregard of propriety. They frequently disrupted church services by abusing and shouting down the preacher. They were also resolute, as were many other sects, in their refusal to pay tithes, the traditional local tax levied for the upkeep of the parish clergy. It is easy to see why contemporaries regarded the Quakers as among the most socially dangerous of the radical groups.

The prayer meetings of the 'Society of Friends' (the Quakers' formal title) took the form of individual believers calling out their thoughts as the Lord inspired them. This invariably involved much physical rocking or quaking, hence their nickname. Such a pattern of worship was obviously open to abuse by the neurotic or those in love with the sound of their own voice, but in practice Quaker meetings seem to have been remarkably harmonious. There was sufficient shared belief to allow such voluble expressions of inspiration on the part of the individual to be accepted by the whole assembly.

It is interesting that the modern Quaker movement should now be strongly identified with pacifism. In the 1650s, it was seen as an aggressive organisation quite prepared to use force when it felt threatened. This may well be the reason why the court lists of the time show so many prosecutions of Quakers and why the magistrates frequently imposed severe sentences on them. Over 2,000 Quakers were brought to trial during the Interregnum. The distinctive style of their speech and their sombre black clothing aroused opposition in the localities. Their refusal to conform to the custom of doffing their hats as a mark of respect, even when brought before magistrates or judges, was hardly calculated to endear them to the civil authorities, who often turned a blind eye when Quakers were set upon, as they frequently were, by the local rowdies.

Cromwell was not opposed to the Quakers over their form of worship; his worry, as with all the religious sects, was not their private beliefs but their public behaviour. If they engaged in disruptive or scandalous practices, this could only delay the process of healing and settling. He was on good personal terms with George Fox, and interceded on occasion to prevent Quakers from being prosecuted without good reason. The notable example of this was his reaction to the notorious case of James Nayler in 1656. In October of that year, Nayler had ridden into Bristol on a donkey, surrounded by adoring women, in apparent imitation of Christ's entry into Jerusalem on the first Palm Sunday. He was arrested for blasphemy by the local magistrates. Fears of widespread Quaker disturbances led to what was in itself a minor local affair being taken up by Parliament, which ordered Nayler to be brought to Westminster. In self-righteous zeal, the House denounced Nayler and sentenced him to a series of brutal punishments, which included a ferocious flogging and the boring through of his tongue.

Cromwell was deeply disturbed, not simply by the savagery of Nayler's treatment, but because be believed Parliament had exceeded its authority. In December he wrote sharply to the Speaker to inform Parliament that nothing in the *Instrument of Government* conferred on them the legal powers they had claimed. His chief anxiety was that Parliament had gone beyond its constitutional rights by denying 'liberty of conscience'.

2 Cromwell and the Sects

> **KEY ISSUE** How tolerant was Cromwell in his dealings with the sects?

Religious considerations weighed heavily with Cromwell, both because of the intensity of his own faith in God, and because he held that the root cause of the civil wars had been religious division. When, as Protector, he spoke of 'healing and settling', he was referring to the need to establish religious harmony in England. His conviction was that the turmoil of the civil wars had been the Almighty's way of preparing England for 'godliness' and religious peace, which it was now the duty of those in government to implement.

Cromwell condemned those religious fanatics who 'press their finger upon their brethren's conscience'. His view was typically and clearly expressed in his defence of a soldier named Henry Warner, who had been cashiered because of his religious views. Cromwell wrote to Warner's commanding officer, Major-General Crawford, a Presbyterian:

1 The man is an Anabaptist ... Admit he be, shall that render him incapable to serve the Public? He is indiscreet. It may be so; in some things, we have all human infirmities. I tell you, if you had none but such indiscreet men about you, and would be pleased to use them kindly, you
5 would find [them] as good a fence to you as any you have yet chosen. Sir, the State, in choosing men to serve them, takes no notice of their opinions; if they be willing faithfully to serve them, that satisfies. I advised you formerly to bear with men of different minds from yourself. Take heed of being sharp, or too easily sharpened by others,
10 against those to whom you can object little but that they square not with you in every opinion concerning matters of religion.[1]

Cromwell believed that religious freedom was a fundamental right, but he was very conscious of the difficulty in bringing the various sects to recognise each other's freedoms.

> Liberty of conscience is a natural right; and he that would have it, ought to give it. Indeed that hath been one of the vanities of our contests. Every sect saith: 'Oh, give me liberty!' but give him it, and he will not yield it to anybody else.[2]

He frequently expressed his dismay that those very people who had joined the struggle against Charles I in order to gain religious freedom for themselves were now denying it to others:

1 Those that were sound in faith, how proper was it for them to labour
for liberty, for a just liberty, that men should not be trampled under for
their consciences! Had not they laboured, but lately, upon the weight of
persecutions? And was it fit for them to sit heavy upon others? Is it
5 ingenuous to ask liberty, and not to give it? What greater hypocrisy than
for those who were oppressed by the Bishops to become the greatest
oppressors themselves, so soon as their yoke was removed.[3]

Cromwell held that unless a particular religious belief led to subversive public behaviour it should be tolerated:

1 Our practice hath been, to let all this Nation see that whatever pretensions to religion would continue quiet, peaceable, they should enjoy
conscience and liberty to themselves; – and not make Religion a pretence for arms and blood; truly we have suffered them, and that cheer-
5 fully, so to enjoy their own liberties. If a man of one form will be
trampling upon the heels of another man; if an Independent, for
example, will despise him who is under Baptism and will revile him and
reproach and provoke him, I will not suffer it in him. If, on the other
side, those of the Baptists shall be censuring the godly ministers of the
10 nation that profess under that of Independency; or those that profess
under Presbytery shall be reproaching or speaking ill of them, slandering them and censuring them – as I would not be willing to see the day
on which England shall be in the power of Presbytery to impose upon
the consciences of others that profess faith in Christ – so I will not
15 endure to reproach them. God give us hearts and spirits to keep them
equal.[4]

Cromwell's appeal for toleration was not simply a matter of words. He
took action to achieve it. Among the ordinances of 1653 (see page 50)
were two notable measures which aimed to bring order to the disputed question of church appointments. The title of the ordinances
gave a clear indication of their purpose: 'An Ordinance for
Appointing Commissioners for Approbation of Public Preachers' and
'An Ordinance for Ejecting Scandalous, Ignorant and Insufficient
Ministers and Schoolmasters'. Between them the Ordinances set up a
body of Commissioners, subsequently known as 'Triers and Ejectors',
who were responsible for the selection and the supervision of those
appointed to public ministries in the church. Significantly, the ordinances made no attempt to prescribe what doctrines were acceptable.
Cromwell's aim was not to persecute particular beliefs but, on the
contrary, to provide greater toleration by removing or debarring
those clerics whose extreme views or behaviour disturbed the religious peace for which he longed. He was anxious that the
Commissioners should be drawn from as many denominations as
possible; Baptists, Independents, and Presbyterians appeared in the
lists of appointees. The evidence suggests that his policy was largely
successful. Even some of the strongest critics of Cromwell's religious

toleration admitted that the work of the Triers and Ejectors had improved the quality of the church ministry. Moreover, in practice, relatively few of the incumbent ministers needed to be removed, since the greater majority showed themselves ready to reform and improve their behaviour.

Throughout the Protectorate, Cromwell was engaged in a balancing act, trying to satisfy the army, whose natural sympathies were with the sects, without alienating Parliament, which became increasingly dominated by conservative Presbyterians as the 1650s wore on. At the same time, he still had hopes of achieving a religious settlement that would usher in godliness and toleration without permitting extremism. During his Protectorate, Cromwell made considerable efforts to ensure that the parish system was maintained and improved. This was because he judged that in the conditions of the 1650s the traditional church structure in the localities had to be preserved if the ordinary people were to have access to the means of worship. This also meant the continuation of tithes for the support of the clergy.

Cromwell's attempt at religious balance created strains between him and his parliaments. His dilemma was that he was invariably more tolerant than they were. As the Nayler case showed, his efforts to hold parliament's repressive tendencies in check were not always successful. He knew that he was engaged in a thankless task:

1 I have had buffets and rebukes, on the one hand and on the other; some
   censuring me for Presbytery; others as an encourager of all the sects
   and heresies in that nation. I have borne my reproach; but I have
   through God's mercy not been unhappy in preventing any one religion
5 impose upon another.[5]

His apparent indulgence of the sects worried the more conservative elements in society. He was referred to mockingly as 'the darling of the sectaries'. One of the most insistent themes in the huge volume of pamphlets published in the 1650s was the need to guard against the threat posed by the religious sectaries. The growing readiness in the late 1650s of the Presbyterians to consider making common cause with the royalists (see pages 105–106) arose not from any great love for Charles II but from a fear of what uncontrolled sectarianism might do. A return to some form of strong, centrally-controlled church authority seemed to offer the best means of uniting against the religious extremists.

It is arguable that, judged against the religious intensity and bigotry of his times, Cromwell was the most tolerant of rulers. He was the first English statesman to make religious toleration the basis of government policy. An interesting example is his giving serious thought in the 1650s to the suggestions that Jews be granted full freedom in England. All this needs to be put in its mid-seventeenth century context. He was not a modern liberal. His toleration was selective and conditional. It did not extend, for example, to Catholicism or what he called 'blasphemy', by which he meant the extreme sectaries. Nevertheless, it was during his Protectorate that England experienced an unprecedented degree of religious freedom.

3 Cromwell and the Royalists

> **KEY ISSUE** Why were the royalists unable to mount an effective challenge to the rule of Cromwell as Protector?

One of Cromwell's constant fears as Protector was that the unsettled situation might encourage a royalist uprising in England. Much of his foreign policy was directed at preventing the Stuarts from finding allies abroad who would be willing to support such a venture. His anxieties are understandable, but with hindsight it can be seen that they were exaggerated. The royalists themselves represented only a minor threat to the Protectorate. It was only when the other conservative forces in England allied with them, something which did not happen until after Cromwell's death, that the restoration of the Stuart monarchy became a possibility.

Following his defeat at the Battle of Worcester in 1651, Charles II fled to the Continent where he remained for the next nine years. His enforced absence left the royalists leaderless and made it very difficult for them to organise themselves into an effective opposition to the republican regimes of the Interregnum. Until 1658, the strength and reputation of Cromwell's army made thoughts of a royalist rising unrealistic. Moreover, there was little backing in the localities for the royalist cause; while few people were enthusiastic supporters of the Commonwealth and the Protectorate, they were not willing to put themselves at risk by openly challenging those in power. Most royalists were cowed by the restrictions that branded them as 'delinquents', imposed heavy fines on them and, in some cases, made their estates forfeit. The introduction by the Major-Generals of a further 'decimation' tax on royalists was largely successful in its aim of convincing them that open support for the Stuarts carried too high a price. The Sealed Knot, the royalist organisation supposedly concerned with planning a Stuart restoration, spent most of its time discouraging uprisings because it feared that their almost inevitable failure would discredit the royalist cause.

The one exception to the pattern was the rising led by John Penruddock in Wiltshire in 1655. It began as an attempt on the part of some royalists in exile to prove that their cause was still alive. Believing that there were potential centres of resistance throughout the country just waiting to be given a lead, they encouraged Penruddock, a former colonel in Charles I's army, to seize Salisbury, an important administrative centre for the West Country. Penruddock duly led a contingent of royalist troops, variously estimated at between

200 and 400, in an attack upon the gaol in Salisbury. The information on which the exiles had based their plans proved woefully inaccurate. Penruddock's attack aroused practically no support either locally or nationally. After only two days, his force was scattered and defeated. Penruddock and the leading conspirators were tried and executed, while a number of the lesser rebels were transported to Barbados.

As significant as the rising itself was the speed with which Cromwell's government responded to put it down. Equally striking was the readiness with which the authorities in the localities reacted, and their ability to raise some 4,000 local militia troops to suppress the rising. It is clear that, although there might well have been considerable latent sympathy for the idea of a return to monarchy, there were few in 1655 willing to put their lives or livelihoods at risk by openly siding with the royalists. This illustrates a characteristic of the period 1640–60 on which modern historians lay great stress – the tendency of great majority of the population towards neutrality. Their natural inclination was to avoid trouble. Sometimes they were drawn by circumstances into affairs which obliged them to take sides, but their choice was frequently more a matter of expediency than of conviction.

Another factor that undermined Penruddock's venture was the quality of the intelligence service upon which the government were able to rely. This contrasted sharply with the inadequate royalist network of communication. Credit for this lies with John Thurloe, Cromwell's Secretary of State. In the tradition of Francis Walsingham, Elizabeth I's great spymaster, Thurloe operated an elaborate espionage system. A constant stream of reports from informers and double agents in Europe, as well as England, allowed him to be always one step ahead of those plotting against the Protectorate. The famous diarist, Samuel Pepys, remarking on the success of Thurloe's spy system, wrote: 'Cromwell carried the secrets of all the princes of Europe at his girdle'. Thurloe's prior knowledge of the royalists' plans helps to explain why Penruddock's Rising was overcome so easily.

A genuine challenge to the regimes of the Protectorate required an organised coalition of all the forces opposed to it. Given the strength of the army, there was little chance of this happening until after Cromwell's death. The key to the survival of the Commonwealth and Protectorate was the loyalty of the army. Although, on occasion, groups within the armed forces expressed hostility towards the governments and parliaments of the 1650s, Cromwell never seriously looked like losing the loyalty of his troops. His successes as a commander since 1641 and his readiness to take up the grievances of his soldiers had endeared him to them. Affection for him and respect for his reputation survived throughout the 1650s. However, the situation changed once his strong hand was removed. The precarious stability that Cromwell had been able to preserve broke down. Factions returned and the struggle over who controlled the executive was renewed.

4 Cromwell as Protector

Cromwell was in a paradoxical position as Protector. He was heir to a

> **KEY ISSUES** What were Oliver Cromwell's aims as Protector?
> How well did he hold the balance between the conflicting
> interests with which he had to deal?
> Was Cromwell a dictator?

revolution but he was not a revolutionary. In all that he did as Protector, he favoured traditional forms. His basic political approach was one of caution. This is well illustrated by his rejection of the offer of the Crown, even though he believed that the best system for England was one that 'had something monarchical in it'. He always sought to work within the constitution as he understood it. He accepted the *Instrument of Government* and the *Humble Petition and Advice*, which placed him under certain constraints. He depended on military power, but was reluctant to use it to impose himself on the nation as a dictator. He occupied a halfway position. Having been instrumental in removing the Stuart monarchy, he was then unwilling to go further and create an entirely new system. Although he was prepared to use force, as in his dissolution of the Rump, it was always as a last resort. When faced by the widespread unpopularity created by the rule of the Major-Generals, he abandoned the experiment.

Cromwell's position as Protector meant that he got the worst of both worlds. On the one hand, he lacked the authority and public acceptance associated with traditional monarchy; on the other, he never pushed his authority to the point where he had a genuine controlling power. What added to the ambiguity of his position was that as Protector he was the hope of many who had supported the parliamentary cause since 1642 in order to create a new order in church and state. Cromwell's disinclination to follow a radical path when in office deeply disappointed them. He was accused of being both a hypocrite and a turn-coat.

'He doth smile and smile even while he smites thee under the fifth rib.' So said a Leveller pamphlet in 1649 by way of illustrating Cromwell's treachery. To those, such as the Levellers and republicans, who found Cromwell's government to be a tyranny both in concept and practice, his hypocrisy was self-evident. However, to those who understood the difficulties in which Cromwell found himself as Lord Protector, trying to exercise balanced yet effective authority, the charge of hypocrisy did not stand. They saw him as being faced with insuperable problems in a time of uncertainty and discord.

What has to be remembered is that Cromwell was so involved with the everyday running of government that he had little time to develop an overall policy. It is doubtful whether Cromwell really knew his own intentions very far ahead. He was essentially an opportunist, who justified his actions after the event by reference to the Lord's divine will. He is recorded as having said that, 'He climbs not so high as he who knows not withersoever he goeth'. Gerald Aylmer sums him up neatly as 'a pragmatist who waited on providence.'

This did not mean that Cromwell was without broad aims. He wanted a godly commonwealth and a 'reformation of manners', by which he meant that in public and private affairs moral considerations should govern behaviour. In social terms, he was very much a conservative. He wanted the traditional strata of society to remain: 'a nobility, a gentry and a yeomanry – that is a good estate', he observed. In religion, he appealed for what he called 'liberty for tender consciences', the right of individuals, provided they were not Papists or blasphemers, to worship God as they saw fit without having to conform to the dictates of an organised church.

It is the broadness of these aims that is most notable. He seldom translated them into clear and specific programmes. Most of his time as Protector was spent trying to control the excessive demands of others. His dissolution of a parliament was usually on the grounds that it had exceeded its authority or was making demands that threatened the balance on which order depended. However, he could not escape the reality of his position. He was Protector because he was head of the army. Try as he might to restore effective civilian government, his authority was basically military. Yet, given the power he held, he was very sparing in its use. In a number of remarkable respects Oliver Cromwell's personal rule was the opposite of tyranny. He tried to make Parliament representative, and to give it a genuine role in the constitution. This is an aspect that impresses modern scholars. Aylmer observes: 'Cromwell had both commanded sufficient following and respect to enable the processes of government ... to continue, and had successfully set about giving his rule a civilian base.'[6]

Yet, no matter how genuinely fair-minded and tolerant Cromwell's policies were, he was in a position to introduce them only because of his military strength. He may have been reluctant to use force, but this could not disguise the fact that he retained the power to do so. As Derek Hirst has pointed out 'He [Cromwell] craved a parliamentary settlement which would secure the liberty of 'men as men'; yet he had also fought for liberty for the Christian conscience, and only the army could guarantee the latter'.[7]

References

1 W.C. Abbott (Ed.), *The Writings and Speeches of Oliver Cromwell*, Cambridge, Mass, 1937–47, vol. I, p. 278.
2 R.G. Richardson and G.M. Ridden (Eds.), *Freedom and the English Revolution*, Manchester UP, p. 31.
3 *Ibid.*, pp. 31–32.
4 W.C. Abbott (Ed.), *The Writings and Speeches of Oliver Cromwell*, Cambridge, Mass, 1937–47, vol. II, p. 535.
5 *Ibid.*
6 G.E. Aylmer, *Rebellion or Revolution*, OUP, 1986, p. 194.
7 Derek Hirst, *Authority and Conflict*, Edward Arnold, 1986, p. 333.

Summary Diagram
Cromwell, the Sectaries and the Royalists

---

the radical sects defined

Baptists   Independents   Congregationalists   Fifth Monarchists
Muggletonians   Seekers   Ranters   Quakers

their threat to the traditional order in church and state

Cromwell's religious attitudes

his relations with the sects   his wish to establish godly government
his belief in liberty of conscience

---

the royalists during the Protectorate

Penruddock's Rising, 1655

royalist weakness

Cromwell as Protector

his relations with the army   his political and religious enemies
the limits of his authority
the extent of his achievements

Working on Chapter 4

Your aim should be to deepen your understanding of, and to develop your own ideas about, the Chapter's four main themes: the radical sectaries, Cromwell's relations with them, the royalist threat during the Protectorate, and an assessment of Cromwell as Protector. The following selection of key points with accompanying questions will provide a useful framework against which to test your understanding of the material.

1. The Sects –
   Why did they become so prominent in the 1650s?
2. Cromwell and the Sects –
   How difficult was it for him to follow his principle of 'liberty of conscience'?
3. Cromwell and the Royalists –
   Why were the royalists unable to mount an effective challenge to the Protectorate?
4. Cromwell as Protector –
   What were the basic difficulties that confronted Cromwell in exercising his authority as Protector?

It would help to understand Cromwell's objectives and difficulties as Protector, if you were to refer to the political analysis in Chapter 3 and to the treatment of Protectorate foreign policy in Chapter 5.

Answering structured and essay questions on Chapter 4

Examples of structured questions that ask you to *describe* some aspect of a person, movement or event:

1. Describe the main beliefs of the following groups: **a)** Fifth Monarchists, **b)** Congregationalists, **c)** Quakers.
2. What problems did Cromwell experience in trying to establish religious toleration during the Protectorate?
3. Describe the efforts made by the royalists to challenge the power of the Protectorate.
4. What were Oliver Cromwell's main aims as Protector?

Examples of structured questions that ask you to *explain* or *make judgements* about individuals, movements or events:

5. To what extent was the character of the Protectorate shaped by Cromwell's objective of achieving 'a godly nation'?
6. How appropriate do you find the description of Cromwell as 'the darling of the sectaries'?
7. In what ways do Cromwell's relations with the radical sectaries illustrate the problems he confronted as Protector?

Each of these three questions calls for an analysis of the constraints that Cromwell placed upon himself by his attempts to extend toleration to the sects. His effort to achieve balance was clearly a crucial factor. The weighting in question 5 is more on Cromwell's own spiritual beliefs. Appropriate reference to his understanding of what 'godliness' constituted is essential here.

8. Why were the supporters of the Stuarts unable to mount an effective resistance to the Cromwellian Protectorate?

9. 'Unrealistic in conception, inept in practice'. How accurate is this as an explanation of the failure of Penruddock's Rising (1655)?

10. How acceptable do you find the assertion that 'the failure of the royalist cause in the 1650s was a matter not of Protectorate strength but of royalist weakness'?

For obvious reasons, examination questions on the royalists in this period tend to concentrate on the theme of failure. You will notice that Penruddock's Rising, even when not specified, is central to each of questions 8, 9 and 10. This is because it was the only major overt challenge to the Protectorate. Consequently, an analysis of the reasons for its failure provides the essential material for all the questions.

11. How accurate is it to suggest that, as Protector, Oliver Cromwell was 'King in all but name'?

12. Examine the view that Cromwell's difficulties as Protector arose from his reluctance to use the power that he had at his disposal.

Oliver Cromwell as Protector is obviously a major examination topic area. You can best approach it by setting yourself a number of sub-questions.

Was his essential aim one of balance? Did he try to play off the political and religious groups against each other? What powers did he actually have at his command? Were there any limitations on that power? In what respects did the authority of traditional monarchy resemble or differ from that exercised by Cromwell? The material you compile from thinking out answers to such supplementary questions can then be used to good effect in tackling questions 11 and 12.

Source-based questions on Chapter 4

1 Cromwell and Liberty of Conscience
Study Cromwell's defence of the Anabaptist on page 74, and his comments on pages 74–75. Answer the following questions:

a) Examine the significance of the following statements made by Cromwell: 'the State, in choosing men to serve them, takes no notice of their opinions' (page 74 lines 6–7). (5 marks)

'Liberty of conscience is a natural right' (page 74). (*5 marks*)
'men should not be trampled upon for their consciences' (page 75). (*5 marks*)

b) Using your own knowledge and the material in the sources, explain why Cromwell was so concerned with the question of religious liberty during his Protectorate. (*15 marks*)

c) How adequate a picture of Cromwell's attitude towards the sects do these sources provide? (*15 marks*)

2 *Cromwell and the Sects*

Study Cromwell's statements on page 75, and then answer the following questions:

a) What religious ideas do you associate with the following groups to which Cromwell refers: 'the Baptists', 'Independency', 'Presbytery'? (*15 marks*)

b) How justified would you judge Cromwell to be in accusing the sects of 'hypocrisy'? For what reasons might he have been particularly sensitive on this issue? (*15 marks*)

c) Using your own knowledge, judge how genuinely Cromwell applied the principle of freedom of conscience to the sects he defines in these sources. (*15 marks*)

5 Foreign Policy During the Interregnum

POINTS TO CONSIDER

A contemporary royalist historian, the Earl of Clarendon, famously wrote that Cromwell's real power lay not at home but abroad. It was certainly the case that England during the Protectorate was held in awe and fear by Continental Europe. It is also true that the policies followed by Cromwell in this period went far beyond his time in their significance. Britain's later development as an empire could not have occurred in the way that it did but for his achievements in foreign affairs. Your aim should be to gain an understanding of the main features of Cromwell's policies by following England's conflicts with Holland and Spain, which are the dominant themes of the chapter. This will put you in a strong position to appreciate the last section which offers an assessment of the character and importance of the Protectorate foreign policy.

KEY DATES

1651	Oct	Navigation Act introduced.
		Charles II escaped to France.
1652	May	Outbreak of the Dutch War.
1653	Aug	Dutch defeated off Texel.
1654	Apr	Dutch War ended.
		Treaty with Sweden.
		Act of Union with Scotland.
	July	Treaty with Portugal.
	Sept	Treaty with Denmark.
	Dec	English fleet sailed against Spanish colonies.
1655	May	English forces failed to take Hispaniola.
		English captured Jamaica.
	Oct	Defensive alliance with France.
1656	Sept	Beginning of war with Spain.
1657	Mar	Military agreement with France.
	Oct	Capture of Mardyke.
1658	June	Battle of the Dunes.
		England acquired Dunkirk.

1 Background

> **KEY ISSUE** How had the Reformation influenced England's foreign policy?

The Reformation, which had begun in the reign of Henry VIII and had been consolidated under Elizabeth I, had made England a Protestant nation. This put her at variance with the Catholic states of Europe, the two most powerful being Spain and France. Spain was viewed as the greater menace, since her Habsburg rulers saw it as their religious duty to lead a holy crusade against such 'apostate' countries as England. There were deep fears among European Protestants that Spain was intent on becoming 'a universal monarchy', for, besides being a leading power in Europe, she had also acquired a great overseas empire by conquering large areas in the newly-discovered Americas. The terrors that Spain aroused in the sixteenth and seventeenth centuries may be compared to the anxieties felt by the West about Soviet expansionism during the Cold War period of the twentieth century.

The unsuccessful attempt of the Armada to invade England in 1588 was the outstanding example of Anglo-Spanish hostility. Ever after, distrust of Spain remained a dominant English attitude, particularly among Puritans. They urged that the nation should forge a European Protestant alliance against Spain. Little came of this during the reigns of the first two Stuarts, since both James I and Charles I chose to avoid foreign entanglements where possible. This angered those Puritan critics who regarded the Stuarts' reluctance to become involved in a Protestant league as evidence of their sympathy with popery. Such bitterness underlay much of the criticism voiced in parliament of royal foreign policy.

Between 1641 and 1648 there had been frequent rumours of royalist plots to bring French or Spanish forces into England to crush Parliament, but none of these had materialised. No foreign country played a direct part in the English civil wars. One reason was that Europe was largely preoccupied with the last stages of the Thirty Years War, which occurred between 1618 and 1648. Initially, this had been a struggle between Catholic and Protestant states but as the war progressed it became increasingly difficult to define it in religious terms. National rather than religious considerations seemed to prompt the actions of the states involved. This became particularly evident from 1635 onwards when the two major Catholic powers, Spain and France, went to war against each other. It was this blurring of the religious issue that confounded the hopes of those English Puritans who expected that, with the abolition of kingship, English foreign policy would become distinctly Protestant again.

The reason why foreign alignments could not be formed simply along religious lines was that concerns other than religion had begun to shape national attitudes. Foremost among these was economics. For more than a century, trade rivalry had been a cause of growing hostility between England and other continental countries. Where religious division and commercial rivalry coincided, as with England and Spain, mutual antagonism was the logical outcome. But it was seldom as simple as that. Religious sympathies and commercial interests did not always match. This was particularly the case with England and Holland (the United Provinces of the Netherlands). As far as religion was concerned, the two countries shared a common Protestantism. Yet this did not create a harmony of interest. Their trade rivalry in Europe and the East Indies and their long-running dispute over fishing grounds tended to take precedence over their religious sympathies. This became especially evident with the ending of the Thirty Years War in 1648, which had the disturbing result for England of leaving the large Dutch merchant fleet free to monopolise the shipping routes in the North Sea and the Baltic.

2 External Affairs during the Commonwealth

> **KEY ISSUES** What was the purpose of the Navigation Act of 1651? Why did the Commonwealth become involved in war with Holland?

The execution of Charles I in January 1649 profoundly shocked all the courts of Europe, Catholic and Protestant. For a time this created hopes among royalists and fears among republicans that there would be pro-Stuart foreign interventions in England. However, Cromwell's rapid subjugation of Ireland and Scotland removed the immediate threat of a successful royalist reaction and enabled the Rump to consider what its attitude should be to the outside world.

One of is first thoughts was that it could strengthen its position internationally by an agreement with the United Provinces. Superficially there seemed to be very good reasons why England and Holland should come together. They were both Protestant, both had a strong anti-Spanish tradition, and they had both very recently become republics. Accordingly, the Rump, expecting that their representatives would be warmly received, sent a special mission to the Hague to discuss the terms of an alliance. But the new English government had failed to grasp the degree of anger aroused by the execution of Charles I. Although Holland was predominantly republican in its outlook, the other provinces still contained a strong sympathy for the House of Orange, which until 1650 had ruled over the Netherlands. The execution in England of the reigning monarch appeared to have greatly troubled them. When the English ambassadors arrived in the Dutch capital, they were subjected to insults and shouts of 'regicides' from the crowds in the streets. Not surprisingly, the mission ended in failure.

a) The Navigation Act, 1651

In his report back to parliament, the Rump's leading ambassador, Oliver St John, roundly condemned the Dutch for abandoning the Protestant cause and for being concerned solely with their own self-interest. He described them as 'juggling sharks'. St John became the chief mover of the Navigation Act, which the Rump then introduced as a way of punishing the Dutch for their refusal to enter into an alliance. There was a further and much stronger motive in that the merchant-dominated Rump was eager to strike a blow against the United Provinces as England's major commercial rival.

The Navigation Act, which was introduced in 1650 and finally passed in October 1651, laid down that all goods imported into Britain from Africa, Asia or the Americas were to be carried only in British vessels, and that exports from Europe were to be admitted into Britain only in British ships or those of the exporting country. This is often referred to as an early example of mercantilism, a form of protection or trade war. The introduction of the Navigation Act was accompanied by the deliberate whipping up of anti-Dutch hysteria. The Rump encouraged the publication of cheap newspapers and broadsheets depicting the Dutch as renegade Protestants, still besotted with monarchy, and corrupted by thoughts of commercial gain. The Dutch retaliated angrily by denouncing what they regarded as English fanaticism and hypocrisy. Open war between the countries became increasingly likely. It needed only a pretext.

b) The Dutch War, 1652–4

This duly came in May 1652 when the Dutch and English fleets encountered each other in the Downs, off the Kent coast. Defying a demand that they respect the English republican flag by lowering their own flags in deference, the Dutch opened fire instead. The war that followed lasted until April 1654. It took the form of a series of naval engagements, fought mainly in the Channel and the North Sea. Initially, the Dutch, led by Admiral Van Tromp, had the better of affairs but, after his death in the Battle of Texel in August 1653, the war turned against them. The emergence of Robert Blake as a naval commander of genius began to give the English a distinct advantage. It was also at this juncture that the Rump government began to benefit from the strengthening of the navy that had been initiated by Charles I. It was a bitter irony for the royalists to have to contemplate.

A series of English victories led to the blockading of the Dutch coast. By December 1653, the Dutch had suffered heavy shipping losses and were willing to make peace. Both sides had good reason at this point for ending the fighting. In Holland, the republicans, under the leadership of John De Witt, had gained the upper hand over the Orangists, the Dutch royalist party. The majority of Netherlanders were now unwilling to continue a ruinous war which, at least in part, was being fought on behalf of the Stuarts. December 1653 also marked a significant political change in England. With the resignation of the Nominated Assembly, whose religious fanatics had been passionately committed to war against the Dutch as betrayers of the Protestant cause, cooler heads began to prevail. Within days of the establishing of the Protectorate peace talks had begun.

3 Foreign Policy under the Protectorate

> **KEY ISSUES** What were the motives behind the Protectorate's 'Western Design'?
> What factors drew Protectorate England closer to France?
> Why did the Protectorate become involved in the affairs of the Baltic states?

a) The End of the Dutch War

Cromwell had been a reluctant supporter of war against Holland. He regarded it as a scandal that Englishmen should be fighting fellow-Protestants. His abiding conviction was that Spain was the great threat. He was fond of remarking that 'the Spaniard is your natural enemy'. Cromwell believed that he was singled out by God to fight the forces of Anti-Christ, whom he identified in Europe as the Spanish. One way to achieve this would be to unite the Protestant nations of Europe in a godly federation. His belief that he had a divine mission to chastise Spain was an extension of his belief that he was God's instrument for achieving a reformation of manners in England.

Newly installed as Lord Protector in December 1653, Cromwell was ideally positioned to respond to the growing desire for peace with the United Provinces. He was aided by the timely revelation that the war had been brought about by Spanish intrigue. Puritan propagandists alleged that Jesuit agents in Holland and England had plotted together to create enmity between the two nations as a means of advancing the universal tyranny of Spain. Pamphlets poured forth claiming to show evidence of the treachery. The striking feature of all this was not the concocted evidence itself but the readiness with which it was believed. Cromwell himself claimed to have personal knowledge of Spanish plots to subvert the English army.

The purported revelations strengthened the argument for an end to the Anglo-Dutch war. The outcome was the Treaty of Westminster, signed in April 1654, under which the Dutch agreed to abide by the Navigation Act, to honour the English fleet at sea, and to cease providing haven to English royalists. Complaints were voiced in

England that the Protector had failed to gain any significant economic advantages from the Treaty. The complaints had substance, for Cromwell at this stage was much more concerned with promoting an anti-Spanish alliance with the Dutch than with enforcing harsh economic terms on them. He was even prepared to offer the Dutch a monopoly of the East India trade if they would wage war on Spain. In the event, the Dutch, although sympathetic to Cromwell's plan, were not yet ready for another war and declined to move against the Spanish.

b) The Western Design and War against Spain

The defeat of the United Provinces considerably enhanced the military reputation of the Protectorate. This encouraged other European nations to consider the advantage of alliance with England. By the end of 1654, the Protectorate had entered into trade agreements with Sweden, Denmark and Portugal. These strengthened Cromwell's determination to challenge the power of Spain. The theatre chosen for hostilities was not Europe but the Spanish colonies in the Americas, hence the later description of it as 'the Western Design'. The essential aim was to capture the Spanish-controlled Caribbean islands and then turn them into permanent bases from which the English could destroy Spain's fleets and so break her empire.

The decision to attack Spain was taken in the weeks immediately following the end of the Dutch war in April 1654. There was no particular provocation to justify the attack but there was a particular opportunity. With the close of the war against Holland, England had at its disposal over 150 warships and their crews. In session with his Council of State, Cromwell discussed the feasibility of using this formidable force to seize the Spanish colonies. Unfortunately for historians, only a portion of the minutes of this Council meeting has survived, and this has raised doubts about what actually took place. One reading of the evidence is that Cromwell took the initiative by urging the Council to undertake an anti-Spanish crusade. He denounced the King of Spain as 'the greatest enemy to the Protestant cause in the world' and argued that England had every right to retaliate for the wrongs done to her people. As he later declared to Parliament:

1 There is no intelligent person but will easily see how empty and weak the reasons are that the Spaniard has for claiming for himself alone an empire of such vast and prodigious extent. The Spaniards endeavour to justify themselves for having enslaved, hanged, drowned, tortured and
5 put to death our countrymen, robbed them of their ships and goods even in time of profound peace and that without any injury received on their part; which cruel usage and havoc as often as the English call to remembrance they cannot miss to think their former glory is quite gone and their ships of war become entirely useless if they suffer themselves
10 to be any longer treated in such a disgraceful manner.[1]

Another interpretation is that Cromwell, rather than leading the Council to its decision, was persuaded by the merchant representatives to adopt a war policy. One complication is that, although for the sake of convenience it is customary to speak of the merchants as if they were a single body of opinion, the truth is that they represented a range of attitudes. There were, for example, merchants who stood to gain greatly from the English seizure of Spain's territories and the takeover of her trade, while there were others, such as the wool merchants, who, because they traded directly with Spain, were unhappy at the prospect of a war involving disruptive embargoes and blockages. It may be that, in deference to this latter group, the decision was made to restrict the war to an attack upon the Spanish colonies and to leave European Spain untouched. There are also strong hints that the Council was not unanimous in its decision. John Lambert, for one, appears to have expressed serious doubts about the proposed strategy.

As with the Dutch war, the prelude to war against Spain was a full-scale propaganda campaign. The enemy was depicted as a ravening beast, intent on destroying Protestant liberties throughout Europe, and imposing the 'universal monarchy' of Spain over the whole world. A torrent of illustrated pamphlets invoked folk memories of the Armada and the Inquisition.

Indeed, greater planning seems to have gone into preparing public opinion for the war than into the actual attack on the Spanish colonies. The broad strategy was clear enough. The large fleet that set sail in December 1654, commanded by William Penn and Robert Venables, aimed to capture the main Spanish-occupied islands in the Caribbean, Hispaniola (modern Haiti) being the principal target. However, the tactics adopted were not well-thought out. The wrong area of the island was chosen for landing, distances were miscalculated, and the troops were decimated by a combination of extreme heat and disease. Spanish resistance also proved determined and effective. The English had to withdraw. Very much as an afterthought, they re-directed their forces into what proved to be a successful attack upon Jamaica.

Subsequent history was to show that, strategically and economically, the island of Jamaica was as valuable a prize as Hispaniola would have been. Its capture could be said, therefore, to have fulfilled the main purpose of the Western Design. At the time, however, it was difficult to avoid the conclusion that the campaign had been largely a failure. Thousands of troops had been lost and, as many merchants had feared, Spain had retaliated to the unprovoked attack on her colonies by closing her European ports to English vessels. The Dutch were prompt to make up for their recent war losses by moving into the trading areas now barred to the English. Another unintended result was that, with the English fleet preoccupied in the Caribbean, piracy, which was an ever-present menace in this period, had a free hand elsewhere. Above all, the campaign was expensive. At a time when the Protectorate was experiencing severe financial problems, the wasteful expenditure on a dubious Spanish war was difficult to justify.

c) Reaction to the Western Design

Initially, Cromwell was distraught at the English failure to take Hispaniola but characteristically he came to terms with it by ascribing it to 'the hand of God'. He interpreted the affair as the Almighty's way of rebuking the English nation for its slowness in adopting true godliness. Besides explaining the failure, this interpretation provided an added justification for his introduction later in 1655 of the rule of the Major-Generals (see page 52).

Cromwell found himself the subject of fierce criticism over the war. One charge was that in his religious zeal he had misunderstood the nature of 'universal monarchy', the main threat of which came, some said, not from Spain but from France. Henry Vane spoke of France as being governed by 'the most tyrannical principles' and being intent upon European domination. Others saw the greater danger coming from Sweden, which, under its powerful monarch, Charles X, had made substantial advances in the Baltic, an area of rapidly expanding commercial importance. One important voice was that of Slingsby Bethel, who believed that Sweden and France represented a joint threat: 'These two countries are like to have divided the Western Empire [by which he meant western Europe] between them'.[2]

Some critics complained that the war had disrupted their trade with Spain. They did not see it as a necessary struggle since Spain was no longer a real power in Europe. They argued that she was a 'lost nation', meaning that her greatness was a thing of the past. We need to appreciate the nature of the commercial objections to the war with Spain. The question of cost was critical. Few were willing to pay the heavy taxes required by the war when the commercial outcome for themselves was loss rather than gain. The Western Design appeared to be pursuing unrealistic religious ends at the expense of hard-headed commercial ones.

d) Cromwell's Colonial Policy

These contemporary criticisms relate directly to a modern debate over whether Cromwell's Western Design constituted an early form of imperialism. Those who think that it did point to the acquisition and settling of colonies and bases from which a trading empire could be spread. Alan Smith goes so far as to describe Cromwell as the founder of the British Empire. He points to the active support given by Cromwell to the English Puritan colonists in North America in their expansion into neighbouring regions belonging to Holland and

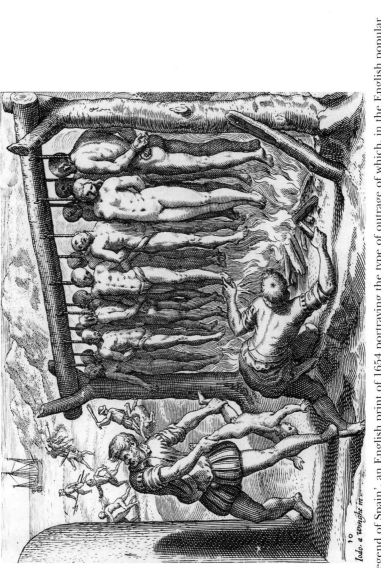

'The Black Legend of Spain', an English print of 1654 portraying the type of outrage of which, in the English popular imagination, Spain was guilty.

France. One example was his dispatch of a naval squadron to seize Acadia (modern Nova Scotia) from the French in 1654. Cromwell was also keen to encourage English emigration to the West Indian islands. After Jamaica was acquired in 1655, it was official Protectorate policy to promote settlement there. Assisted passages and guaranteed land rights were offered as inducement.

There was no great rush to take up such offers. The only significant number of settlers who went to Jamaica and the other islands in the 1650s were prisoners sentenced to transportation and orphans obliged to serve as indentured apprentices. Judged by this measure, the Protectorate's colonial settlement policy would appear to have had little impact. However, the argument of those historians who still regard it as significant is that, regardless of its immediate failure, the policy established a vital precedent. For the first time in English history, central government had undertaken the responsibility of promoting organised overseas settlement, rather than leave it as a matter of individual or group enterprise. Thus the basis for imperial expansion had been laid.

Some historians have interpreted Cromwell's foreign policy with its extension of British claims overseas as a sign of the influence of the bourgeoisie (the commercial middle class), who were eager to develop their trade and commerce. However, this line of reasoning has been challenged by other scholars who have doubted whether Cromwell ever thought in terms of establishing a trading empire. Steven Pincus regards the Western Design not as a means of establishing overseas territories, but as a device for breaking the power of Spain by denying her resources from her American colonies.[3] Other historians have also pointed out how difficult it is to reconcile the view of Cromwell as an agent of the bourgeoisie with those aspects of his policy where he followed religious aims regardless of whether they served England's commercial or economic interests. The problems he experienced throughout his Protectorship with the merchants hardly supports the notion that he was their representative.

e) Relations with France

Cromwell, while acknowledging that France was a Catholic power, was impressed by the willingness of the Bourbon monarchy to tolerate the Huguenots (French Protestants). Despite whispers that this toleration was more honoured in the breach than in the observance, Cromwell was convinced by his cordial personal relations with Cardinal Mazarin, the French Chief Minister, that France would make a better ally than an enemy. When the war with Spain brought England only limited gains, Cromwell was drawn even closer to the idea of an agreement with France. The French were eager. They had been hoping for some time to win the new English government to their side in their long-running war with Spain.

⁊❧ By the Protector.

A PROCLAMATION

Giving Encouragement to such as shall transplant themselves to *Jamaica*.

Whereas the Island of Jamaica in America, is by the Providence of God, in the hands and possession of this State, the Enemy which was found upon it, being fled into the Mountains with an intention to escape into other places, (save such of them as do daily render themselves to our Commander in chief there, to be disposed of by him; and We being satisfied of the Goodness, Fertility, and Commodiousness for Trade and Commerce of that Island, have resolved, by the blessing of God, to use Our best endeavours to secure, and plant the same. For which end and purpose, We have thought it necessary to publish, and make known unto the People of this Commonwealth, and especially to those of the English Islands, Plantations and Colonies in America, our Resolutions and Intentions on that behalf, as also to declare unto them the Encouragements which We have thought fit to give unto such as shall remove themselves, and their habitations into the aforesaid Island of Jamaica, within the time mentioned and expressed in these Presents. And first, concerning the securing thereof against the Enemy, We have already upon the Island, which landed there in May last, above six thousand Souldiers, and the beginning of July after, We sent from hence a Regiment of eight hundred more, drawn out of Our old Regiments in England, with eight Ships of War, besides Victualers, to be added to twelve others, that were left there by General Pen, under the command of Captain Will. Goodson, all which are appointed to remain in those Seas for the Defence of the said Island; and We shall from time to time take care to send thither other, both Land and Sea Forces, that We may have allwaies in those parts, such a strength as may be able, though by the blessing of God, to defend and secure it against any Attempt of the Enemy; that whereas the Planters in other places have been at Great and vast expences at their first sitting down, and in the very beginning of their Plantations for their necessary defence, aswell against the Natives of the Countrey as other Enemies, those who shall remove thither, will be under the immediate Protection of this State, and so eased both of the danger and charge which other Plantations are subject to, and shall have, for their further encouragement, the terms and conditions following.

1. Those who shall transport themselves as aforesaid shall have land set forth unto them, according to the proportion of twenty Acres, besides Lakes and Rivers, for every Male of twelve years old and upwards, and ten Acres for every other Male or Female, in some convenient place of the said Island; and in case any whole Plantation, That is to say, the Governours and greatest part of the people shall remove themselves, they shall be preferred in respect of the place of their sitting down, that it may be near some good Harbour commodious for Commerce and Navigation.

2. That the said Proportion of Land shall be set forth unto them, within six weeks after notice given by them under their hands, to the hands of some of them on the behalf of the rest, unto his Highness Commander in chief, or Commissioners there, appointed for that purpose of their resolutions to remove, and of the time they intend to be upon the place.

A Proclamation promoting English emigration to Jamaica
The second paragraph reads:
Those that transport themselves as aforesaid shall have land let forth unto them, according to the proportion of twenty acres, besides lakes and rivers, for every male of twelve years old and upwards, and ten acres for every other male or female, in some convenient place of the said Island; and in case any whole Plantation, that is to say, the governors and greater part of the people shall remove themselves, they shall be preferred in respect of the place of their setting down, that it may be near some good harbour commodious for commerce and navigation.

The path to better Anglo-French relations was eased by French co-operation over a notorious incident in 1655. In May of that year, the Protectorate government learned of the massacre of hundreds of Protestants in the Alpine Vaudois valley, carried out by the troops of the Duke of Savoy. Cromwell, acting as the defender of the persecuted Protestants of Europe, protested angrily to the Duke:

1 Oliver, Protector, to the most serene Prince Emmanuel, Duke of Savoy, Prince of Piedmont, greeting: We understand that such of your Royal Highness's subjects as professed the reformed religion are commanded to depart their native habitations and that when they applied to your
5 Royal Highness for a revocation of the edict, a part of your army fell upon them most cruelly, slew several, put others in chains and compelled

the rest to fly into desert places and to mountains covered with snow, where some hundreds of families are reduced to such distress that tis greatly to be feared they will in a short time perish through cold and
10 hunger. These things when they were related to us, we could not choose but be touched with extreme grief and compassion for the sufferings and calamities of this afflicted people and we most earnestly beseech your Royal Highness that you would command their losses to be repaired and that an end be put to their oppressions.[4]

Cromwell appealed for support to France, an ally of Savoy. The French obliged by applying diplomatic pressure on Savoy, with the result that the persecution of the Protestants in the area was halted. This highly co-operative response on the part of France was a further step towards an Anglo-French agreement, which was duly reached in October 1655 in the shape of a defensive alliance. One considerable gain for Cromwell was that France agreed that it would no longer give shelter to the Stuarts.

England, a Protestant power, was now in alliance with France, a Catholic power, against Spain, another Catholic power. Clearly, the alignment could not be explained on religious grounds. National prestige and economic rivalry seem to have been more important factors. In March 1657, the original Anglo-French alliance was transformed into a military agreement. Under it its terms, Protectorate troops joined French forces in an attack upon Spanish Flanders. Decisive allied victories came with the capture of Mardyke in October 1657 and at the Battle of the Dunes in the following June. One result of this latter victory was that England acquired the port of Dunkirk. The war with Spain outlived Oliver Cromwell and was not finally ended until May 1659 when France and Spain made peace in the Treaty of the Pyrenees.

f) The Baltic Question

The Protectorate's dealings with the Baltic powers was a further example of the difficulty in the 1650s of trying to base foreign policy on purely religious considerations. Cromwell had marked personal respect for Charles X, the Swedish King, and hoped that their two countries might form a Protestant union. Cromwell also judged that it was necessary for England, as a trading nation, to have a direct involvement in Baltic affairs. The growing commercial importance of the Baltic region made this essential. Neither the Protector nor the Swedish King was happy with the growing influence of the Dutch in the area. In 1654, Sweden and England entered into a treaty intended to weaken the Dutch grip upon trade and to counterbalance an existing treaty between Holland and Denmark. Since all four of these countries were Protestant, religious considerations can hardly be said to have been of any relevance in their relations. There was certainly no sign among the Scandinavian and Baltic nations that they were prepared to suspend their economic rivalry for the sake of a Protestant league against the likes of Spain or France.

Although Charles X frequently expressed commitment to the Protestant cause, he appears to have done this largely to retain English support in his difficult relations with his Baltic rivals, an aim which proved largely successful. In 1655 and again in 1657, when Sweden was in danger of being opposed by a combination of other Baltic states, Cromwell was prepared, against the wishes of the pro-Dutch lobby in England, to provide Charles X with both ships and money. However, in the last year of Cromwell's life, there were signs that he had begun to doubt the value of the Anglo-Swedish connection and to fear that Sweden was becoming too powerful in the Baltic. Richard Cromwell adopted the same attitude during his brief period as Protector. During a further Baltic crisis in 1658–9 he supported Denmark and Holland in their resistance to Sweden's control of the Sound, a vital waterway which gave access to the Baltic. Richard declared that England would not tolerate such a threat to the free passage of her merchant ships. In the event, Sweden backed off, but Richard's response was taken by many as clear proof that his father's pro-Swedish policy had been based on a misreading of the situation.

4 The Debate on Cromwell's Foreign Policy

> **KEY ISSUES** What were the aims and principles behind Cromwell's foreign policy?
> How successful was Cromwell in achieving his aims?

In describing foreign policy during the Interregnum, historians have tended to fall into one of two camps: those who see it as basically a continuation of the traditional anti-Catholic policy dating from the time of Elizabeth I, and those who regard it as a new progressive policy in which commercial considerations predominated. The weight of modern opinion is that Cromwell's policies were essentially dated: in a world that had rapidly changed into one of commercial competition, he still clung to an Elizabethan idea of a post-Reformation religious alignment. The obvious example is his attitude to Spain. Spain was declining as a world power and her place was being taken by France, yet Cromwell persisted in giving priority to what he perceived as the Spanish threat. This accounts for the quarrel that he then had with the merchant representatives in parliament. They pointed out that to persevere with policies based upon dubious interpretations of religious interests was to endanger England's far more important economic concerns.

During the 1650s relations between the European states were never simply a matter of religious affiliation. Catholic France remained at war with Catholic Spain, Protestant England fought against Protestant Holland, and Protestant Sweden went to war first with Catholic Poland and then with Protestant Denmark. Such complexity doomed any attempt to follow a purely religious line in foreign affairs. There are strong grounds for suggesting that by the end of the Thirty Years War in 1648, secular considerations had began to take precedence over religion in shaping national attitudes. That is why Cromwell's sincere attempts to forge a Protestant alliance appear anachronistic.

A question which interests many modern historians is how much authority Cromwell exercised personally over the shaping of foreign policy. He was, of course, the outstanding figure of his time and there has been an understandable tendency to think of him as the initiator of the policies of the Protectorate. Certain historians, notably Barry Coward, are anxious to point out that the evidence suggests that he was not always a free agent.[5] The pressures he imposed on others were probably balanced by those he felt himself to be under.

Perhaps modern analysts try too hard to determine the principles underlying Cromwell's foreign policy. It is doubtful that he ever had the luxury of conducting his policy according to a predetermined plan. It is much more likely that he framed his policy on a day-to-day basis, conscious that circumstances required immediate responses. In 1656, the Venetian ambassador in London recorded the strain borne by Cromwell and his Council: 'They are so fully occupied they do not know which way to turn, and the Protector has not a moment to call his own'. Cromwell was trying in a very brief period of time to adapt to a complex and changing diplomatic and military situation in Europe. Therefore, it is somewhat unrealistic for later historians to attempt to distinguish between religious, commercial and national motivation in his policy.

It should be stressed that Cromwell had little experience of foreign policy before he became Protector. Commenting on Cromwell's approach to foreign affairs, Slingsby Bethel remarked dryly that the Protector 'was not guilty of too much knowledge of them'. Cromwell's outlook towards other countries was, therefore, conditioned by the prevailing Protestant English distrust of Catholic nations. However, as Protector he was the guardian of the nation's overseas interests. This obliged him to temper his prejudice with the realities of the European diplomatic situation. He never entirely lost his conviction that Spain was uniquely evil, but circumstances forced him to acknowledge that other nations also represented a threat, whether religious or commercial, to English concerns.

England's military reputation among foreign nations grew so greatly under Oliver Cromwell that throughout the period of the Protectorate the English royalists had no genuine chance of gaining allies in Europe who were willing to risk supporting an attempted Stuart restoration. English diplomats, who had been often treated with disdain in Europe in the early years of the Commonwealth, found themselves respected and courted in the days of the Protectorate. Andrew Marvell, the poet, wrote that Cromwell 'once more joined us to the continent', while Samuel Pepys, the diarist, declared that 'he made all the neighbour princes fear him'. The royalist historian, Clarendon, made a remarkable summary of Cromwell's achievements:

> 1 To reduce three nations, which perfectly hated him to an entire obedience, to all his dictates; to awe and govern those nations by an army that was indevoted to him, and wished his ruin was an instance of a very prodigious address. But his greatness at home was but a shadow of the
> 5 glory he had abroad. It was hard to discover which feared him the most, France, Spain, or the Low Countries.[6]

Yet, the Protectorate's national prestige was bought at a heavy domestic price. Foreign policy proved extremely costly. Maintaining naval squadrons was a drain on already limited resources and Cromwell's attempts to raise grants for their upkeep increased the tension between him and his parliaments.

In one area Cromwell clearly failed. His dreams of a Protestant federation against Spain came to nothing, largely because European politics had changed. As the later stages of the Thirty Years War had shown, religion was no longer the major determinant of international relations. Cromwell's slowness to appreciate this led him to persevere with policies that in many respects were out of date.

Cromwell's Western Design was only a partial success, but it paved the way for a French treaty. Although, in one obvious sense, alliance with a Catholic power compromised his original concept of a Protestant crusade, it enabled him to gain greater protection for the Huguenots and the Vaudois Protestants. The alliance also led in time to England's regaining Dunkirk, a toe-hold in Europe at the expense of Spain. It is also arguable that, whether intended or not, the Western Design marked the beginning of a colonial policy that in time would lead to the creation of the British empire.

References

1 W.C. Abbott (Ed.), *The Writings and Speeches of Oliver Cromwell*, Cambridge, Mass, 1937–47, vol. III, p. 891.
2 Stephen Pincus, 'England and the World in the 1650s', in John Morrill (Ed.), *Revolution and Restoration: England in the 1650s*, Collins and Brown, 1992, p. 146.
3 *Ibid.*
4 W.C. Abbott (Ed.), *The Writings and Speeches of Oliver Cromwell*, Cambridge, Mass, 1937–47, vol. III, p. 719.
5 Barry Coward, *Oliver Cromwell*, Longman, 1991, pp. 168–74.
6 G.Huehns (Ed.), *Selections from Clarendon*, OUP, 1966, p. 358.

Working on Chapter 5

To understand foreign policy you need a working knowledge of the main features of the international scene. That is why it is worth making sure you have grasped the principal ideas in the Background section. Two themes dominate the period: England's wars with Holland and Spain. Use sections 1 and 2 to acquaint yourself with the origin and outcome of these wars. Cromwell is so significant a figure that it is important to gain an understanding of the debate that still surrounds his foreign policy. This is best done by following the treatment in section 3, which analyses his relations with Spain, Holland, France and the Baltic states, and then studying the assessment of his aims and achievements, which appears in the final two sections.

Summary Diagram
Foreign Policy During the Interregnum

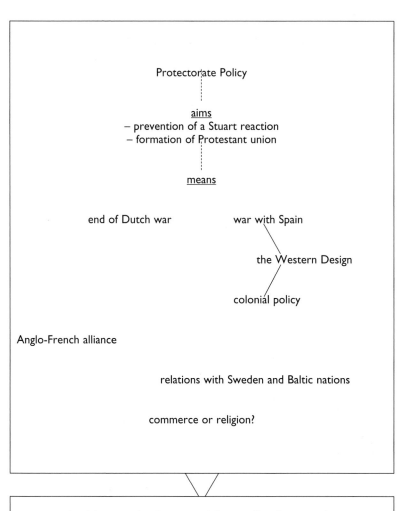

Commonwealth Policy
the shock of Charles I's execution
the Navigation Act, 1651
war with Holland, 1652–4

Protectorate Policy

aims
– prevention of a Stuart reaction
– formation of Protestant union

means

end of Dutch war   war with Spain

the Western Design

colonial policy

Anglo-French alliance

relations with Sweden and Baltic nations

commerce or religion?

the debate on the character of Cromwellian foreign policy

Answering structured and essay questions on Chapter 5

Structured questions:

1. What were the main terms of the Navigation Act of 1651? What did England hope to gain from the Act?
2. Describe the steps that led **a)** to the end of war with the United Provinces in 1654, and **b)** to the outbreak of war with Spain in 1656.
3. What benefits did England derive from the Anglo-French agreements of 1655 and 1657?

Essay Questions:

Conrad Russell, one of the major modern authorities on the period, has suggested that the reason why Protectorate foreign policy receives such a large amount of attention from historians is because it makes an excellent subject for examination questions. His wry comment has a serious and consoling aspect, for there is indeed a self-contained character about the subject that should make it attractive to the student. Exam questions most frequently ask about the motivation behind Protectorate policy. Consider these typical examples:

4. How accurate is it to say that the Dutch war of 1652–4 failed to serve English interests?
5. 'The Western Design was grander in concept than in achievement.' How acceptable do you find this assessment?
6. 'There was never a single Protectorate foreign policy, only a number of separate policies'. How acceptable do you find this suggestion?
7. To what extent was foreign policy during the Protectorate determined by commercial considerations?
8. How far do you agree with the view that Cromwell's foreign policy was based on outdated principles?
9. 'Aggressive coloniser' or 'Protestant zealot': which is the more appropriate description of Oliver Cromwell in his conduct of foreign policy? Give reasons in support of your choice.
10. What grounds are there for regarding Oliver Cromwell's foreign policy as 'having laid the base for British imperialism'?

Although the questions differ in form, the essential thrust is the same in each. What is being sought is an analysis of the underlying aims of Protectorate policy. The list divides into two groups: questions 4 to 7 deal with the Protectorate broadly, questions 8 to 10 with Oliver Cromwell directly. Your task is to judge the weighting to be given to your material. This will vary from question to question. One of the persistent weaknesses in exam answers is their failure to be relevant to the particular question being tackled. Compare questions 7 and 9. Obviously there is a considerable overlap of material, but test yourself by deciding which of the following points should go into each answer: England's desire to protect and expand its trade, Cromwell's bitterness against Spain, his hopes of a Protestant union, English enmity towards the Spanish empire, the unsuccessful attack upon Hispaniola and the taking of Jamaica, England's relations with France and Holland, merchant objections to the Western Design, the degree of Cromwell's personal involvement in the Design, and encouragement of colonial emigration.

Source-based questions on Chapter 5

1 The Spanish Question
Study Cromwell's assertions on page 90 and the illustration on page 93. Answer the following questions.

a) Explain Cromwell's reference to 'an empire of such vast and prodigious extent' (lines 2–3, page 90). (*5 marks*)
b) Using your own knowledge and the evidence in the illustration, describe the main features of 'the black legend of Spain'. (*10 marks*)
c) In what ways do these two sources contribute to an understanding of why the Western Design was undertaken? (*15 marks*)

2 The aims of Protectorate Foreign Policy
Study Cromwell's letter on page 96 and the Proclamation on page 95, and then answer the following questions.

a) Using your own knowledge and the evidence in the Proclamation, explain the developments that led to Jamaica becoming an area of British immigration in the 1650s. (*10 marks*)
b) How would you explain the tone and style adopted by Cromwell in his letter to the Duke of Savoy? (*10 marks*)
c) Using you own knowledge, explain how Cromwell's appeal to the Duke of Savoy contributed to the development of improved Anglo-French relations. (*15 marks*)
d) How useful are the Proclamation and the appeal as evidence of the character of Protectorate foreign policy? (*15 marks*)

6 The Path to Restoration, 1658–60

POINTS TO CONSIDER

It is important not to read history in reverse and assume that there was a logical, if not inevitable, drift towards monarchy during the two years after Oliver Cromwell's death. The predominant feature was the uncertainty of the times. The contending groups were clearer about what they did not want than about what they did. Opportunism rather than clearly thought-out strategies became the order of the day. As in any situation where the political system is weak or confused, the power of the sword predominated. Much as the civilian and religious groups may have disliked the presence of the military, it was the army that held the key to any settlement. This had been true since the execution of Charles I in 1649. That truth was re-emphasised in the period following Oliver Cromwell's death. Protector Oliver may not have been overwhelmingly popular, but even his opponents had admired his military prowess. As long as he was at the helm, disorder had been contained. But with his passing nothing was certain anymore.

The many twists and turns of this period make it a complex one. To avoid becoming confused, try to keep to the chronology of events. You will be able to do this if you follow the five-theme analysis adopted in this chapter:

1 The Protectorate of Richard Cromwell, September 1658–April 1659,
2 The Restored Commonwealth, May 1659–February 1660,
3 The Restored Long Parliament, February–March 1660,
4 The Convention Parliament, April–May 1660,
5 The Restoration of Monarchy, May 1660

KEY DATES

1658	**Sept**	Death of Oliver Cromwell.
		Richard Cromwell became Protector.
1659	**Jan–Apr**	Third Protectorate Parliament.
	Apr	Richard Cromwell resigned – end of the Protectorate.
	May	The Commonwealth restored – Rump re-assembled.
		End of Spanish war.
	Aug	Booth's Rising.
	Oct	The Army expelled the Rump.
	Oct–Dec	Government by Committee of Safety.
		Widespread disturbances throughout England.
	Dec	Rump re-assembled.
1660	**Jan**	Monck's troops crossed from Scotland to England.

Feb	Monck's troops reached London.
	Return of excluded members to the Rump.
	Rump dissolved.
Mar	Long Parliament restored.
Apr–May	Convention Parliament.
Apr	Lambert's army defeated at Edgehill.
	House of Lords re-convened.
	Charles II issued Declaration of Breda.
	Both Houses voted to accept Declaration of Breda.
May 8	Charles II proclaimed King.
May 29	Charles II entered London.

1 The Protectorship of Richard Cromwell, September 1658–April 1659

> **KEY ISSUE** Why was Richard Cromwell's Protectorship so short-lived?

In September 1658, under the terms of the *Humble Petition and Advice*, Richard Cromwell duly succeeded his father as Lord Protector and Commander-in-Chief. Great as Oliver Cromwell's difficulties had been, he had managed to preserve an uneasy balance between the demands of army, the religious radicals and the traditionalists. But he had been able to do this only through his personal authority and power. The permanence he had sought had eluded him. He had not created the new form of self-sustaining civilian government that he so much desired. The Protectorship that he bequeathed to his son was dependent on the willingness of the army to continue supporting it.

Richard Cromwell inherited a situation which contained four main political groupings: the army, the republicans (Common-wealthsmen), the Presbyterians, and the radical sectaries. To these could be added a fifth element, the royalists. Although they had been subdued during Oliver Cromwell's time, his death and the diffidence of the new Protector encouraged them into action again. What gave the royalists hope was that the Presbyterians who had been greatly disturbed by the disruptive sectaries had become more reactionary in their attitude. The Presbyterians had never been wholly reconciled to the republic; the religious settlement which they had hoped for had not materialised. They were quite prepared, therefore, to consider alliance with the royalists, not out of love for monarchy, but because the alternative was social disorder and religious factionalism.

Another important political factor was the lack of unity among the army leaders. Charles Fleetwood and a number of the senior officers wished to maintain the Protectorate, since, with an inexperienced

Protector, they felt they would be able to control the situation. However, the lower ranks tended to side with the sectaries, who were unhappy with a Protector who seemed to have distinct Presbyterian sympathies. This grouping of soldiers and sectaries called for a return to the Commonwealth, which would mean a return to 1653 and a reinstating of the Rump Parliament.

How deep Richard Cromwell's Presbyterianism went is difficult to judge, but his uneasy relationship with the army certainly led him to rely increasingly on civilian advisers of a conservative outlook. Richard's besetting weakness as Protector was that he was not a solider. Hitherto, he had lived as a country squire, showing little aptitude for either military or political affairs. He now found himself thrust deeply into both. Unlike his father, he could not call on the natural loyalty of the army. This left him only one recourse, to turn towards the civilian elements in government.

The difficulty of Richard's relations with the military soon showed itself when they urged him to give up his position as Commander-in-Chief. At first he refused, which brought fierce criticism from the leading generals, Desborough and Fleetwood. Richard tried to counterbalance this by cultivating the more sympathetic officers. He had some success; Whalley and Gough, who had ruled as Major-Generals in 1655, and George Monck, the Commander of the English army of occupation in Scotland, were some of the more notable officers who sided with Richard.

However, the bulk of the army was not to be won over. There was still deep resentment over the perennial problem of arrears of pay; the total owed to the troops was £900,000. This was an aspect of the overall financial difficulties of the Protectorate. It was falling increasingly into debt. At the beginning of 1659, this was calculated at £2,500,000. The Protectorate's expenditure continued to run ahead of its revenue. The situation was not made any easier by the general economic depression that England was experiencing. One particularly disturbing feature of this was the high price of food, which followed a series of poor harvests and a severe trade recession in the late 1650s. As had his father and Charles I before him, Richard was obliged to call parliament in order to raise money.

a) The Third Protectorate Parliament, January–April 1659

Given the conflicting opinions it represented, Parliament was unlikely to prove co-operative towards Richard. Since there was no formal party system corresponding to the various political groups, it is not easy to give precise figures, but, in a House of 549 members, pro-Protectorate conservatives seem to have been in the majority. Unfortunately for Richard, the republican minority proved much more active and vociferous; it launched into a series of attacks on the legitimacy of the Protectorate. The republicans' main aim was to arouse support among the army. Fearing that such tactics would play into the hands of those who wanted to tighten the military's grip on affairs, the Presbyterian MPs attempted to undermine the army's power. They introduced a resolution that the Council of Officers should sit only with the permission of Parliament, and voted to take the command of the local militia out of the hands of the army and bring it under direct parliamentary control. Officers and ranks united in the face of this and demanded that the Protector dissolve Parliament. Richard resisted, but, when he learned that England was on the verge of an army insurrection, he eventually gave way and did as he was bidden.

Little was now left of this authority. It was clear that he wanted to move towards a predominantly civilian administration by reducing the influence of the army, but it was equally clear that the military would not allow this. With the Parliament dissolved against Richard's wishes, power was effectively back in the hands of the Council of the Army, some of whom, including Fleetwood, were prepared to allow the Protectorate to continue, provided it left the army in charge. However, in order to make their power appear somewhat less stark, the Council recommended the recalling of the Rump, a move that was highly pleasing to the Commonwealthsmen, who felt that their republican agitation was obviously having an effect.

The Rump re-assembled in May 1659. The end of the Protectorate was not long delayed. Richard Cromwell, having tried unavailingly to summon loyal troops from Ireland and Scotland, resigned and withdrew from public life. Three factors explain his failure as Protector: his inability to fashion a government free of army control, the strength of the republican campaign against the Protectorate, and the financial bankruptcy into which his government sank. Richard Cromwell was not especially incompetent, but effective government in the situation created by his father's death required a leader of extraordinary talent. Richard Cromwell was not extraordinary; he was a stolid, honest, squire, who lacked the political skills that the times demanded.

2 The Restored Commonwealth, May 1659–February 1660

> **KEY ISSUES** Why were neither the royalists nor the religious and political radicals able to exploit the situation to their advantage? What role did General George Monck play?

a) The Rump Recalled, May–October 1659

The resurrected Rump soon showed itself to be the same in character and attitude as when it had been dispersed six years earlier. It refused to acknowledge its dependence on the army, with whose leaders it was soon at odds, and behaved as if the events of the intervening six years had never taken place. It denounced the army's interference in political matters, and claimed legitimacy as the only authority representing constitutional continuity. The army was told that its duty was to obey the Parliament it had restored. The faint possibility of this happening disappeared when the army leaders learned that the Rump had no intention of giving priority to their requests for reform. They were especially angered by the Rump's failure to deal with the question of the troops' arrears of pay. The truth was that the two bodies regarded each other as little more than a regrettable necessity. The Rump knew that to preserve itself in troubled times an army was necessary to maintain the peace. For its part, the army appreciated that the Rump served to clothe what would otherwise be recognised as naked military rule.

The irony was that in the country at large the Rump was thought to be too radical. What encouraged this idea was that in a number of counties the restored Rump had tried to curb the influence of the army by deliberately putting the local militia into the hands of the extreme sectaries, including Fifth Monarchists, Quakers and Baptists. This strange development excited fears of a takeover by the religious fanatics. There were even rumours that the Levellers were re-organising. The outpouring of pamphlets in 1659 gave the superficial impression that the radical forces were much stronger than they were. It was this that frightened the conservatives into retreating further towards a restoration of the old constitution.

Something approaching national panic occurred. There was talk of Church and State being under threat. It was in this disturbed atmosphere that a series of scatted Presbyterian-royalist risings took place in the summer of 1659. These were less a genuine attempt to restore the Stuart monarchy than an outburst of irritation at what the Rump was allowing to happen. The government acted quickly. Forewarned of the conspiracies, they were able to break them with a series of military strikes.

The one serious challenge was in Cheshire, where, in August 1659, Sir George Booth held large parts of the county in defiance of the Rump. Booth did not actually call for a return of Charles II, but for a 'free parliament'. This amounted to much the same thing, since it was believed that a freely-elected parliament would be the prelude to a royal restoration. But the fact that he did not openly advocate Charles II's return shows how relatively weak the monarchists still were at this point. It was the disgruntled Presbyterians rather than the royalist supporters of Charles who were making the challenge, thus suggesting that it was more an expression of anti-Rump sentiment than a genuinely pro-Stuart movement. Booth held on for a number of weeks, but his expectation that Spanish troops would arrive to assist him proved unfounded and he eventually surrendered.

There now seemed to be an opportunity for the radicals to establish a hold on England. The Presbyterians and their conservative allies had been broken, and the army had again shown itself able to overcome any royalist challenge. However, the radicals were too ill-defined a group to constitute a single source of opinion, let alone power. The divisions between the religious sectaries, who still hankered after the rule of the saints, and the republicans, who wanted a single-chamber secular parliament, prevented a unified radical approach. There was something very unreal, therefore, about the long debates over possible constitutional change that occupied so much of the Rump's time in the summer and autumn of 1659. The truth was that no settlement could satisfy the wide range of political and religious opinions among the radicals. Still more important, no settlement stood a chance of being adopted unless it first met with the approval of the army.

The crushing of Booth's rising had been directed by John Lambert. His success put him back in the political limelight. He became the hero of the rank and file in the army's growing dispute with the Rump. Lambert gave his support to an army petition which demanded that the Rump's authority be reduced by the creation of a Senate (upper house) and that all the army leaders be promoted to the rank of general and confirmed in their command. The petition also insisted that the army be granted authority to purge all those local corporations that had not actively opposed the recent royalist risings. The Rump interpreted this as a direct attempt by the army to usurp political authority. Arthur Haselrig moved that Lambert and his fellow petitioners be removed and imprisoned. The animosity between Lambert and Haselrig, who were respectively the leading military and civilian republicans, was an indication of how far republicanism was from being a cohesive movement. Haselrig hoped that there were still enough troops faithful to Parliament to prevent an army coup. But he had miscalculated. Retaliation came quickly. In October, regiments loyal to Lambert occupied London and forcibly dissolved the Rump.

b) The Committee of Safety, October–December 1659

There was now nothing to hide the reality of military rule. The army had previously brought down the Protectorate; it had now broken the remaining link with the old constitution. England was again without a legitimate government. Authority lay with the Council of the Army. In an attempt to give its power the semblance of legality, the Council appointed a 'Committee of Safety', composed of the officers and a few token civilians, to act as an interim government until a more permanent body could be established.

The Army Council's dispersal of the Rump had been swift and effective, but it had not won the unanimous support of the army. This was soon evident in the reaction of General George Monck, the Commander in Scotland and someone destined to become the critical figure in the events leading to the Restoration. Monck protested at the dissolution of the Rump. He negotiated with the members of the expelled House, who offered him the post of Commander-in-Chief and invited him to bring his army south to London. Monck prepared to do so and issued a justification for his action; he claimed to have received:

> a call from God and his people to march into England, to assist and maintain the liberty and being of parliaments, our ancient constitution, and therein the freedom and rights of the people of these three nations from arbitrary and tyrannical usurpation.[1]

The Army Council first tried to dissuade Monck from continuing his march. When this failed, they despatched Lambert north to intercept him. But Lambert's forces were no match for Monck's in either morale or discipline. They disintegrated with scarcely a fight.

Monck's protest at the Rump's dissolution and his easy victory over Lambert gave a considerable lift to the forces opposed to army rule. The internal divisions within the army encouraged serious challenges. Widespread disturbances occurred between October and December, notably in Bristol and London. Portsmouth, an important garrison town, declared against the government. So, too, did the navy. It was as if all those unhappy with the prevailing system were now prepared to risk openly challenging it. The Committee of Safety was taken aback by the sheer scale of the pent-up anger that expressed itself. The seriousness of the disorders in London may be gauged from the following description from a newsletter published in December, 1659:

> 1 Yesterday we had a sad day by reason of some bloodshed among us by the soldiers. A petition was on foot by the apprentices to be delivered to the Council, which, coming to the knowledge of the Committee of Safety, they made a Proclamation against it, which was proclaimed yes-
> 5 terday morning in Cheapside by some troopers, who were beaten back by the apprentices, which occasioned the bringing in ... of all the horse and foot of the army into the City, who came with their swords drawn and pistols cocked against a multitude of naked men, and killed 6 or 7, and wounded more; but that did not quiten them, till about 5 o'clock
> 10 the Lord Mayor made proclamation that they should all depart, the soldiers being withdrawn, some of them being killed and wounded. The petition was delivered into the court of Common Council by five young men, who referred it to a Committee to give them answer, and those 6 Alderman and 12 Commoners to consider the safety of the City in
> 15 this juncture of time ... This day my Lord Mayor and Court of Aldermen were sent for to come to the Committee of Safety; but my Lord thought it not good to leave the City at this time of danger, but sent 6 Aldermen to them, who spoke plain English to them.[2]

Protest petitions poured in to the Committee of Safety and to the City of London. Monck was also inundated with petitions as he made his way south. The three commonest themes in all of these were the grim economic circumstances of the day, the tyranny of army rule, and the need for the restoration of ancient liberties through a free parliament or monarchy.

1 Since the death of the King, we have been governed by tumult; bandied from one faction to the other; this party up today, that tomorrow – but still the nation under, and a prey to, the strongest. So long as this violence continues over us, no other government can settle the nation than
5 that which pleases the universality of it. You speak of the necessity of a republic. We say it is not necessary, not even effectual, but if it were both, a free parliament ought to introduce it. The consent of the people must settle the nation, the public debt must be secured out of the public stock, and interests of opinion and property must be secured by a free
10 parliament.

(from a Petition of the Gentlemen of Devon)[3]

That the fundamental laws of England, the privileges of Parliament, liberties of the people, and property of goods may be defended, according to the declaration of Parliament when they undertook the war, and no taxes or free quarter imposed without authority of Parliament.[4]

(from a Request of the inhabitants of the county of Leicester)

1 Our glory and comfort consist in our privileges and liberties, the inheritance of all the free people of England, the grand privilege being free representation in Parliament without which we are no better than vassals.
5 This dear privilege has been assaulted by violence and artifice, heavy taxes are imposed on men's estates, and new laws on our persons without consent of the people in a free Parliament. Trade is decayed and we are like to suffer much.
We therefore beseech you ... by your zeal to our liberties, by the
10 great renown you have lately gained in opposing the cruel raging of the sword, by the common cries of the people ... to use the great advantages God has put into your hands to secure your country from dangerous usurpation and preserve us in the liberties to which we were born.[5]

(from a Petition of the apprentices and young men of London)

Rather than face a renewal of civil war, Fleetwood and the army officers bowed before this storm of opposition. They allowed the Rump to re-assemble in December 1659. This fulfilled Monck's immediate objective, but he continued his march south. His troops crossed the Scottish-English border on New Year's Day 1660 and reached London in February.

c) The Recalled Rump, December 1659–February 1660

What the second recalling of the Rump showed was the deep unpopularity of the army's rule up to that point. The paradox was that army authority could be removed only by the exercise of further military power. None of the civil institutions was capable in itself of resisting the army. The re-installing of the Rump in December could not have been achieved without the intervention of Monck. It was his action that had forced the Committee of Safety to dissolve itself and permit the Rump's reassembly.

The climb-down of the army leaders caused a major political shift; the conservative forces began to recover. Desborough, Lambert and Fleetwood were dismissed by the Rump, and Monck was invited to become Commander-in-Chief. The Rump now appeared to be in a strong position. It had removed the army leaders, re-established itself as a parliament and government and had the backing of Monck, the most powerful general in the land. However, it then proceeded to throw away its advantage by a series of fatal mistakes. Instead of tackling the nation's most pressing grievances, the Rump seemed intent on settling old scores. It undertook a purge of the army. Half the serving officers were removed. Whatever the justice of this, the vindictive spirit in which the purge was carried out and the corruption and nepotism that accompanied the appointment of new officers and officials did not speak well for the integrity of the Rump. Its growing unpopularity was evident in a widespread refusal by traders and merchants to pay parliamentary taxes.

The Rump further revealed its ineptitude in the way it treated Monck after his arrival in London in February. Rather than honouring him as its saviour, which he undoubtedly was, it sought to restrict his influence politically by burdening him with the policing of London, which was still in a highly volatile mood. However, Monck refused to be overawed; he did use his troops to bring order to the City, but he was not to be deterred from involvement in the politics that had brought him south in the first place. He insisted that the Rump confirm the promise given to him that it would not sit beyond May 1660. More significantly still, he outmanoeuvred those MPs who claimed that the Rump was now the sovereign power by forcing the House to re-admit the 'secluded' members – those who had been debarred at the time of Pride's Purge in 1648.

3 The Restored Long Parliament, February–March 1660

> **KEY ISSUE** What impact did the return of the secluded members have on the political situation?

Monck's insistence that the secluded MPs be permitted to retake their seats had striking results. The return of a substantial number of members of the pre-1649 Long Parliament altered the political balance. Although their ranks had been thinned by death over the intervening ten years, they were still a large enough group to tilt the scales against Haselrig's republican faction. Since they had not been implicated in the trial of Charles I or the creation of the Commonwealth, they represented a direct constitutional link with 1642. The claim of the Rump and of the Army Council to direct events had rested ultimately on the legitimacy of Pride's Purge and the execution of the King. Allowing the secluded members to return amounted to a denial of that legitimacy and made a restoration of the Stuart monarchy much more likely. The first steps towards this were soon taken when Parliament turned the tables by excluding the most committed republicans from its ranks. Lambert was a prominent victim of this purge.

Monck was careful at the time the Long Parliament was recalled not to declare openly that he was working for an eventual royal restoration. He wanted to avoid pressing the issue too early. He presented himself very much as the moderate, who, while being resolute against extremists, was prepared to tolerate all forms of responsible opinion. He persuaded Parliament to keep its promise to make him Commander-in-Chief, to appoint a new Council of State, and then, having made preparations for elections for a new parliament, to vote for its own dissolution. Another push towards a royal restoration was given by the Long Parliament's reappointment of Edward Montague, a former Cromwellian general but now a royalist sympathiser, as Commander of the Fleet. This meant that the two leading military commanders, on land and at sea, now favoured Charles II's return.

The tide was running strongly towards a Stuart restoration. Whether this had been Monck's intention all along remains uncertain, but it is significant that as early as the previous July he had entered into a very cordial correspondence with the exiled Charles II. Charles's trust in Monck was clearly expressed in a letter he wrote early in their negotiations:

1 I am confident that George Monck can have no malice in his heart against me; nor hath he done anything against me which I cannot easily pardon, and it is in his power to do me so great service, that I cannot easily reward, but I will do all I can; and I do authorise you to treat with
5 him; and not only to assure him of my kindness, but that I will very

liberally reward him with such an estate in land, and such a title of honour as himself shall desire, if he will declare for me, and adhere to my interest.[6]

4 The Convention Parliament, April–May 1660

> **KEY ISSUE** Why did Lambert fail in his attempt to preserve the republic?

While the elections for the new Parliament were being held, Lambert made one last bid to save the republican cause. He attempted to halt the movement towards a royal restoration by a show of force. A number of regiments supported him, but the bulk of the army declined to challenge Monck. Fleetwood and Desborough made no move; neither did Haselrig, the leading civilian republican. In an ironically appropriate final engagement at Edgehill, the site in 1642 of the first of the civil war battles, Lambert's army was defeated and he was captured.

Monck had overcome the republicans militarily. The election results now showed that his mixture of tact and firmness had undermined them politically. Although the writs for the election had specified that no known royalists were to stand, this was widely ignored; over 60 monarchists took seats in the new House. In contrast, republicans and supporters of the Commonwealth did badly. This was not unexpected. What it proved was that the holding of genuinely free elections encouraged the return of members with royalist sympathies.

The new Parliament, known as the Convention Parliament, gathered on 25 April. The House of Lords was re-convened and the joint Houses then considered the terms for restoration which Charles had previously offered in his Declaration of Breda issued on 4 April.

5 The Restoration of Monarchy, May 1660

> **KEY ISSUE** How much did the successful restoration owe to the way in which Charles II conducted himself?

In a sense, all Charles II needed to do after Monck's dramatic entry into English politics six months earlier was to wait and do nothing. He had shown himself adept at this. His inaction proved decisive for it carried the impression that he was not seeking to impose himself upon the nation but was awaiting their invitation. His Declaration of Breda showed the same shrewd political judgement. The Declaration, said to have been drafted by Clarendon, Charles's chief adviser in exile, was a skilful act of conciliation, based on an astute perception of the outstanding grievances of the time and how they could be

GEORGE MONCK

-Profile-

1608	born to a landed Devonshire family
1625–37	took part as a mercenary in various European wars
1637–41	fought against the rebels in Scotland and Ireland
1642–44	fought as a royalist
1644	imprisoned by Parliament
1646	joined the Parliamentary side
1647–49	with Parliament's forces in Ulster
1650	fought alongside Cromwell at Dunbar
1651	C-in-C of Parliament's army in Scotland
1652–54	a Commander of the Fleet during the Dutch wars
1653	elected to Parliament
1654–58	C-in-C of Parliament's army in Scotland
1659–60	played an increasingly influential role in preparing the way for the Restoration
1660	marched into England
	became Commander of whole Parliamentary army
	negotiated with Charles II
	escorted the King to London for his coronation
	became Duke of Albermale
1665–66	responsible for law and order in London during the Great Plague and Great Fire
1667	fought in the naval war against the Dutch
	made First Lord of the Treasury
1670	died

George Monck's colourful and dramatic public life could be said to have begun in 1625 when he ran away to join the army in order to avoid being arrested for physically assaulting a county sherrif. As a mercenary soldier on the Continent he learned and honed his miltary skills. These he used to effect during the English Civil War, fighting first for the royalists before changing sides and joining Parliament's forces. In Ireland and Scotland, he fought alongside Cromwell, whom he came greatly to admire. Left by Cromwell to carry out the settlement of both those countries, Monck proved to be as able and strong an administrator as he was a soldier. On the death of Cromwell in 1658, Monck supported Richard, believing that a continuation of the Protectorate offered the best chance of stability. But he was never committed to any particular form of settlement purely on grounds of theory. What he wanted was a return of order.

Monck's greatest achievement came in the disturbed period between the end of the Protectorate and the the Restoration. His mixture of firmness and political discretion enabled him to keep the republican and religious extremists at bay and to play the role of go-between in the negotiations between Parliament and Charles Stuart. It is difficult to think of any other contemporary who could have achieved what Monck did. His combination of military strength and political judgement made him an indispensable figure. It is a fascinating irony that it was Monck, a soldier and a Cromwellian, who was chiefly responsible for the resoration of civilian government and monarchy in 1660.

resolved. Charles promised a general pardon, religious toleration, and accepted the right of Parliament to decide the disputed questions of property entitlements and the army's arrears of pay. The key passages read:

1 We do grant a fee and general pardon to all our subjects ... Let all our subjects, how faulty soever, rely upon the word of a king, solemnly given by this present declaration, that no crime whatsoever, committed against us or our royal father before the publication of this, shall ever
5 rise in judgement, or be brought in question, against any of them, to the least endamagement of them ...

And because the passion and uncharitableness of the times have produced several opinions in religion, by which men are engaged in parties and animosities against each other ... we do declare a liberty to tender
10 consciences ...

And because, in the continued distractions of so many years, and so many and great revolutions, many grants and purchases of estates have been made to and by many offices, soldiers and others, who are now possessed of the same, and who may be liable to actions at law upon
15 several titles, we are likewise willing that all such differences, and all things relating to such grants, sales and purchases, shall be determined in parliament, which can best provide for the just satisfaction of all men who are concerned ...

And we do further declare, that we will be ready to consent to any
20 Act or Acts of Parliament to the purposes aforesaid, and for the full satisfaction of all arrears due to the officers and soldiers of the army under the command of General Monck.[7]

Both Houses voted to accept the Declaration as the constitutional basis for the restoration of the monarchy. On 8 May 1660, England was formally declared to be no longer a republic; government again resided in King, Lords and Commons. On 14 May, a parliamentary deputation visited Charles to invite him to retake his throne. On 29 May King Charles II made a ceremonial entry into London.

6 Reasons for the Failure of the Republic

> **KEY ISSUE** Why had the republic been unable to establish itself
> as a permanent system of government?

Within two years of Oliver Cromwell's death in September 1658, the
Stuart monarchy had been restored in the person of Charles II. In
one obvious sense, this was a triumph of the royalist cause, but it
would be wrong to assume that it was simply royalist strength that
brought it about. Indeed, only ten months before Charles's return as
King in May 1660, the royalist rising led by George Booth had been so
poorly supported that it was said that Charles had despaired of ever
regaining his throne. The reasons for the Restoration are, therefore,
to be found less in royalist pressure than in the failure of the republic to resolve the difficulties and contradictions that had dogged it
since its inception in 1649, and which became particularly pro-
nounced after Oliver Cromwell's death. In Austin Woolrych's words:

> 1 The fast rising flood of enthusiasm for the monarchy and the ancient
> constitution expressed a hankering for security and the rule of law.
> Both had suddenly become fragile, indeed, had almost perished in the
> autumn and winter of 1659–60. The Restoration was necessary to fill a
> 5 political vacuum, for the Commonwealth had collapsed inwards,
> destroyed by its own internal strife.[8]

a) The Political Weakness of the Republic

Paradoxically, Oliver Cromwell's problem as Protector was that,
despite the military power on which he could depend, he had not
been prepared to use force to impose a settlement to his liking. He
had maintained his belief that godly rule could be achieved by relying
on the goodwill of honest men. Similarly, after 1658, although the
army frequently interfered in affairs, it never did so with sufficient
sense of purpose to achieve a lasting settlement. The army leaders
remained the final arbiter since no solution would work that was not
acceptable to them, but this was a negative power; it did not guarantee that a solution could be found. The army could destroy, but it
could not create. Moreover, there was serious disunity among the
military. This had also been the case under Oliver Cromwell, but his
authority had been enough to maintain obedience. Without him, the
conflicting attitudes among the officers became much more evident.

The monarchy was restored because the republic had discredited
itself. The Protectorate created in 1653 had attempted to establish a
workable system of government based on a written constitution. With
the abandonment of the Protectorate in 1659, there was a power
vacuum, which the successive regimes were unable to fill. Lacking

constitutional credibility, and sustained only by the authority of an increasingly divided army, the republic had no claim on the nation's loyalty. In the end the forces of conservatism proved stronger than those of radicalism.

b) The Unpopularity of Army Rule

What the period 1658–60 showed was that military rule was unwelcome to the majority of those in positions of social and political influence. For one thing, it was hugely expensive. The cost of maintaining the army and navy meant the retention of heavy taxation, one of the grievances that had previously done so much to poison the relations between King and Parliament. No political settlement that involved the maintenance of high taxation would be acceptable to the established classes. London is a striking illustration of this. Ever since 1640 the capital had been one of the most dependable sources of parliamentary strength; throughout the 1650s it had backed the various governments of the Commonwealth and Protectorate. However, in 1659, large numbers of Londoners had become so embittered by the costs of military rule that they were willing to contemplate a return to monarchy. It was no mere coincidence that the first serious civilian challenge to the army came with the protest of the London apprentices against the Committee of Safety, and the organised tax boycott by the London merchants, in the autumn of 1659.

c) The Contribution of Monck

George Monck's particular skill was in being able to play the role of a moderate throughout the period leading up to the Restoration. This made him acceptable to that growing body of opinion that after nearly 20 years of unresolved turmoil wanted peace and social stability. He could have made a bid for personal power but chose not to; he seems to have genuinely wanted a civilian government. This is very reminiscent of Oliver Cromwell; however, like Cromwell's, Monck's ability to influence events rested on his command of a reliable army. It was again the paradox of an army leader using his military authority to impose a civilian settlement. It could not have been achieved any other way. Without Monck, the royalists would not have been able to recover in the way that they did.

d) Disunity within the Army

A dominant characteristic of the army in the period after Oliver Cromwell's death was its lack of unity. There was rivalry among its leaders and unrest among its troops. The outstanding example of this was the disintegration of Lambert's forces when sent by the Committee of Safety to prevent Monck's march southwards. Their condition typified that of many of the regiments – unpaid, badly provisioned, and reluctant to obey the orders of squabbling commanders. The chief complaint of the lower ranks was that the generals had yet to meet the two demands that the troops had been making since the civil wars began – full settlement of arrears of pay and indemnity against prosecution for deeds done in the wars. It was ironic that, in the end, it was the return of Charles II that resolved these grievances. His promise of pay and indemnity, guarantees which the generals had not been able to deliver to their men in nearly 20 years of fighting, made monarchy appealing even to the rank and file.

e) The Attraction of Monarchy

Few people are wedded to constitutional forms on grounds of pure principle. Self-interest largely determines whether or not a particular system is acceptable. A republic that appeared to increase rather than lessen the financial burdens on the nation and to have no answer to the great social, political and religious questions of the day was finally judged to be not worth preserving.

In contrast, by 1660, a restored monarchy offered the hope of a return to political and religious stability, the end of the army's intrusion into civil affairs, and the re-establishment of the authority of the traditional ruling classes in central and local government. These were sufficiently powerful incentives to convince all but the most extreme religious or political radicals that the republic had outlived its usefulness. 'The old order was the natural order.' This was the basic reason why the restoration occurred. All the other experiments had failed. None had been able to achieve stability or gain acceptance. All had been imposed and all had depended on the power of the army to maintain them.

References

1 H. Tomlinson & D. Gregg, *Politics, Religion and Society in Revolutionary England, 1640–1660*, Macmillan, 1989, p. 229.
2 C.H. Firth (Ed.), *The Clarke Papers*, Longman, 1901, pp. 166–67.
3 Mary Ann Everett Green (Ed.), *Calendar of State Papers, Domestic Series, 1659–60* 13, Kraus Reprint, 1965, p. 331.
4 *Ibid.*, p. 336.
5 *Ibid.*, pp. 344–45.
6 F.J. Routledge (Ed.), *Calendar of the Clarendon State Papers*, Clarendon Press, 1882, vol III, pp. 344–45.
7 John Kenyon, *The Stuart Constitution*, CUP, 1986, pp. 331–2.
8 Austin Woolrych, *England without a King 1649–1660*, Methuen, 1983, p. 46.

Summary Diagram

The Path to Restoration, 1658–60

the factors

army disunity	radical weakness	conservative strength

the contending factions

the army	the republicans	the Presbyterians
the sectaries	the royalists	

the steps along the path

the end of the Protectorate Sept 1658–April 1659

- Richard Cromwell's struggles with the army
- Difficulties with Third Protectorate parliament, Jan–April 1659
- Richard abdicates April 1659

the Restored Commonwealth 1659–60

- Rump recalled, May–Oct 1659
- Booth's Rising, Aug 1659
- Committee of Safety, Oct–Dec 1659
- Monck's intervention
- widespread disorders, riots in London
- Rump again recalled, Dec 1659–Feb 1660

towards a Restoration

- Monck's march to London, Jan–Feb 1660
- Long Parliament reconvened, Feb–Mar 1660
- Declaration of Breda, April 1660
- Convention Parliament, April–May 1660
- Restoration of Monarchy, May 1660

Working on Chapter 6

The central question addressed in this chapter is why the monarchy was restored less than two years after Oliver Cromwell's death. There are two distinct aspects: the narrative of events, and the possible explanations for them. The titles of the sub-sections and the Key Issues provide you with the main signposts in the story, so they are worth adopting as the main points of the narrative. In studying the explanations for the Restoration you would find it helpful to compile two lists, covering a) republican weaknesses, and b) royalist strengths. Again, the Key Issues will guide you in this. The following questions relating to the various chapter sections should help you order and direct your thoughts.

1. Why was Richard Cromwell unable to overcome the problems he inherited as Protector?
2. Why were the Rump's relations with the army so strained?
3. Why were neither the radicals nor the royalists able to exploit the situation to their advantage?
4. How far did the army lose control of events in December 1659?
5. Why did John Lambert gain so little support in April 1660?
6. Was the Restoration inevitable after February 1660?

Answering essay questions on 'The Path to Restoration, 1658–60'

Although questions on this period may vary in emphasis, they tend to revolve around the central issue of why the republic collapsed in the period 1658–60.

Structured Questions:

1. What problems confronted Richard Cromwell as Protector?
2. Describe the main steps taken by the restored Rump to reimpose its authority between May 1659 and February 1660.
3. In what ways, in the period 1659–1660, did General Monck help prepare the way for the restoration of the Stuart monarchy?
4. What steps did Charles II take to ease the path to his restoration in 1660?

Essay questions:

5. How far do you agree with the view that 'the problems that Oliver Cromwell left behind him meant that his son's Protectorate was doomed from the start'?
6. Royalist strength or republican weakness: which do you regard as the more important factor in explaining the Restoration? Explain your choice.
7. Examine the role played by the army in the period between the death of Oliver Cromwell and the restoration of Charles II.

8. How acceptable do you find the claim that 'without Monck there would have been no Restoration'?

9. Explain why it was that the royalist cause failed in August 1659 but triumphed in May 1660.

10. How accurate is it to describe the period from September 1658 to May 1660 as one of 'chaos'?

11. Why did republicanism have so few defenders in England by May 1660?

12. Examine the claim that 'it was the 20 months after Oliver Cromwell's death that really showed how powerful he had been as Protector'.

Since they relate to a concentrated period of barely two years, there is considerable overlap between the questions. Your task is to judge the different weighting and emphasis that the questions require. For example, questions 6, 9 and 11 are concerned with assessing the respective strengths and weaknesses of the royalists and republicans. Questions 7, 10 and 12 call for an overview of the whole period covered by the chapter, which means that you would have to be selective in your material in order not to become lost in detail. Questions 7 and 8 have obvious overlaps; however, 7 is concerned with the full 20 months after September 1658, while 8 is directed particularly at the events from December 1659 onwards. Oliver Cromwell is specifically mentioned in 5 and 12, but ask yourself – are they primarily about him? A little reflection should suggest to you that the answer is that they are not. The technique being used in the question here is the familiar one of throwing light on a period by referring to what had gone before. You are being asked to assess the character of the years 1658–60 by contrasting it with the relative stability of the preceding period. Of course, you need knowledge of that earlier time (consult Chapters 3 and 7) to make the comparison, but the focus is on the period 1658–60.

Consider question 11. An effective approach would be for you to draw up a list of the weaknesses of the republican cause; these might include lack of unity among the political and military republicans (Haselrig and Lambert illustrate this point well), their failure to seize their opportunities earlier in the 1658–59 period, and their military weakness as shown by Lambert's inability to challenge Monck. It would then be appropriate to describe the growing strength of the royalist reaction by May 1660; Monck is obviously important here, as is the broad movement towards a return to the original constitution among all but the radicals, who were a dwindling influence by 1660. A key point to emphasise is that, by May 1660, republicanism was largely discredited. It was perceived to have had 11 years in which to find the answers to the nation's problems, and to have failed. As the response to Charles II's Declaration of Breda showed, monarchy was deemed to have far more to offer in 1660.

Source-based questions on Chapter 6

1 The Challenge to Army Rule
Study the newsletter on page 110 and the petitions on page 111.
Answer the following questions:

a) What picture of the unrest in London can be drawn from the newsletter? (*5 marks*)
b) How far do the petitions express a common set of grievances? (*10 marks*)
c) How useful is this collection of sources to the historian who is seeking to understand the reasons for the recall of the Rump in December 1659? (*10 marks*)
d) To what extent does the evidence in these sources suggest that the collapse of the republic was imminent? (*15 marks*)

2 Monck and the Restoration
Study Monck's declaration on page 110, Charles II's letter on pages 113–14 and the Declaration of Breda on page 116. Answer the following questions:

a) Using your knowledge and the evidence in Monck's declaration and the King's letter, identify the motives that led Monck to march into England In January 1660. (*10 marks*)
b) Analyse the significance of the following terms as they appear in the Declaration of Breda:
'liberty to tender consciences' (lines 9–10, page 116 (*5 marks*)
'all arrears due to the officers and soldiers' (line 21, page 116). (*5 marks*)
c) How far does your understanding of the Declaration of Breda lead you to accept the suggestion that 'it showed Charles II's realistic grasp of the outstanding grievances of the time'? (*15 marks*)
d) Using your own knowledge and the evidence in these sources, comment on the assertion that the Restoration owed less to Monck's action than to Charles II's inaction. (*15 marks*)

7 Conclusion: The Interregnum in Historical Perspective

POINTS TO CONSIDER

Historians continue to differ in their assessment of the Interregnum. Some modern scholars argue that its real significance lies in what it discredited. Others see the period less negatively and suggest that in many respects it was a time of major achievement. But whatever line they take, historians agree in regarding the Interregnum as an extraordinary period whose mixture of reaction and experimentation demands analysis. This chapter offers a series of key points in that analysis as a way of providing you with a framework for assessing the character and importance of the 11 years without a king. So, as you read the chapter, try to develop your own opinions about the significance of the period.

The Restoration settlement that followed the accession of Charles II in 1660 attempted to obliterate all that had happened since 1649. The execution of the surviving regicides and the grisly disinterring and public hanging of Oliver Cromwell's body were intended to symbolise the expunging of an unworthy period of history. The Interregnum was to be regarded as an aberration. This was how the royalist chroniclers wished it to be. But too much had happened during the Interregnum for it simply to be dismissed as an unhappy memory.

Although monarchy was re-established it was not a complete restoration of royal power. Christopher Hill has memorably pointed out that, after the events of 1649, English monarchs 'never forgot that they had a joint in their neck', meaning that royal absolutism was now no longer possible. 1660 was as much a restoration of parliament as of monarchy. Charles II was always aware of this and was careful never to push his differences with Parliament too far. When his brother, James II (1685–8), ignored the lessons of the Interregnum and tried to reimpose royal absolutism, he lost his throne. 'The Glorious Revolution' of 1689 which saw William III accept the Crown on the terms laid down by Parliament was the certain end of any notion of absolute monarchy.

The Interregnum also established the place of Parliament as a central and necessary part of the constitution. This may appear an odd claim in view of the chequered history of the parliaments of those years. The forcible expulsion of the Rump in 1653, the contempt in which the Nominated Assembly came to be held, and the unhappy relations of the two Protectors with their Parliaments, none of which ran their full term, hardly suggest that it was a time of success. But the notable thing is how persistent Oliver Cromwell was in his belief that

Parliament was an essential institution. He may have declared that all constitutional forms were 'but dung and dross in comparison of Christ', but he never wholly abandoned the attempt to find one that worked. This was because he accepted that the only alternative to Parliament was unfettered military rule. It is also highly significant that it was Parliament that invited Charles to return to the throne in 1660. In doing this, it gave practical expression to the theory that henceforward Parliament's relations with monarchy would be a matter of partnership rather than subservience.

The fundamental flaw in all the governments of the Interregnum was that their authority rested on a seizure of power, in the form of Pride's Purge and the execution of the reigning monarch. Thereafter, none of them could claim to rule by consent; all of them were imposed. Scarcely 10 per cent of MPs had accepted parliament's right to put Charles I on trial. Moreover, modern estimates suggest that none of the regimes that held office between 1649 and 1660 had the genuine support of more than 10 per cent of the population. Consequently, they governed solely in terms of their own asserted authority. They could not legitimately claim to represent the nation. The break with tradition implicit in the abolition of monarchy meant that they could not ground their authority in precedent.

This would not have mattered had any of the regimes of the Interregnum been genuinely revolutionary. But the persistent argument of the Commonwealth and Protectorate governments was that their rule was in keeping with 'the ancient constitution'. Indeed, they repeatedly claimed that they were restoring the fundamental laws and liberties of the nation. But this claim was undermined by the reality of the situation. Events between 1649 and 1660 showed that Britain never became fully reconciled to military rule. It is clear that the traditional propertied classes wanted a return to civilian authority. The localities were unhappy with the attempts at centralising that occurred in the 1650s. This was most clearly shown in the unpopularity of the Major-Generals and in the local resistance to the idea of centrally imposed taxation; the 'decimation' tax and the 'assessments', raised to maintain the army, were particularly resented.

The experience of the 1650s gave England a strong distaste for standing armies. None of the governments of the Commonwealth and Protectorate was able to make itself independent of the military. Oliver Cromwell aimed to return England to secure and stable civilian government, but the paradox was that to achieve this he had to use military means. He had to employ the very system he was endeavouring to abandon. That was one of the reasons why he gave serious thought to the offer of monarchy in 1657; kingship would have enabled him to detach himself constitutionally from reliance on the army. In an interesting parallel, General George Monk, the architect of the restoration, had come to believe by 1659 that the only effective way in which military rule could be ended was by a return to traditional monarchy, the system under which the executive authority was independent of army control.

Military regimes are invariably highly expensive and it was in this regard that the governments of the Interregnum were at their weakest. The civil wars between King and Parliament had been in part a dispute over the right of the monarch to impose financial levies on his subjects. It was, therefore, ironic that the Commonwealth and Protectorate governments should have had to resort to methods of raising revenue that were even more severe than those the Long Parliament had protested against before 1642. The insuperable difficulty for both the Rump and the Protectorate was that they never had enough money. Faced with this, they resorted to various revenue-raising schemes, which succeeded only in making the regimes who tried to impose them highly unpopular.

If finance was one insoluble difficulty during the Interregnum, religion was another. The failure of the various Protectorate Parliaments to carry the nation towards godly rule, and the fear that the wilder sectaries inspired in the hearts of moderates and traditionalists in this period, combined to suggest that religion was a destructive force when applied to politics. The Interregnum destroyed the idea that England might ever become a confessional or theocratic state. Religion would certainly remain a major factor in British politics after the Restoration, but no serious attempt would again be made to base government purely on religious principles.

Notwithstanding its internal problems, England experienced one of its most notable periods as an international power during the Interregnum. Its defeat of Holland and Spain and the extension of its overseas territories were extraordinary triumphs. In addition, the Protectorate period was one of considerable commercial expansion. In some respects, this was a by-product of the various wars in which England engaged. Although these were presented as religious crusades, the effect of the defeat of the Dutch and the Spaniards was to secure England's control of the seas, giving its merchants access to all the disputed trading regions in the known world. The same expansion occurred in colonial affairs. Indeed, many historians regard this period as marking the beginning of Britain as an Empire.

The Interregnum was, therefore, more than simply a break in the continuity of traditional kingship, and it would be unhistorical to assess the period only by what it destroyed. Important advances were made in administration: finance, law and local government all underwent significant development. Despite the apparent failure of the rule of the Major-Generals, relations and communications between London and the provinces were made smoother. In this context, care needs to be taken not to overstate the power of central authority in these years. The reality was that central government lacked the bureaucratic machinery to enforce its will. It was always dependent upon the co-operation of the traditional ruling authorities in the localities. Furthermore, the evidence drawn from the wide research into local history reveals how marked was the continuity of magistrates and officials in the local community. It was never Cromwell's intention to usurp what he regarded as the 'natural' authority of the local governing classes. Indeed, his aim was to forge a harmony of interest between the Protectorate and the community. In this, he again showed his basic social conservatism.

Oliver Cromwell was, of course, the dominant figure of the period. If there is one thing that his career during the Interregnum illustrates, it is that good intentions are not enough. His hope that, after the traumas of the civil wars, the nation would abandon discord and adopt godly government proved unrealistic. Religious bitterness and political strife did not end with the execution of the King; they became even more intense.

There has long been a major historiographical debate over whether the years 1640–60 constituted a revolution. Indeed, a leading contributor to that debate, Gerald Aylmer, entitled one of his books *Rebellion or Revolution?* What can be said is that, even if the years from 1640 to 1649 are interpreted as a revolution, since they led to the execution of the reigning King and the abolition of monarchy, the following 11 years did not consolidate that revolution. Despite the excitement and fears created by the religious sectaries and political radicals, the predominant feature of the Interregnum was the strength and persistence of conservative attitudes. Few of those in positions of real influence after 1649 wanted to challenge the existing social order. Their criterion for judging the worth of the constitutional experiments introduced during the Interregnum was how well they protected the established order from social disruption. There is little doubt that the political and religious radicalism of the times frightened the nobility and the gentry and made them determined to resist the extension of rights to the lower orders. Thus, the events of the Interregnum, far from encouraging social revolution, made the conservative classes more conservative still. John Morrill summarises the impact in these terms:

1 The English Revolution consolidated the elite when it might have destroyed it; consolidated order by giving everyone a taste of, and distaste for, disorder; prepared the way for the collapse of the confessional State while discrediting the Puritan dream of a godly
5 commonwealth.[1]

However, this reversion to conservatism does not in itself prove that the Restoration was inevitable. Monarchy was not necessarily seen as the guarantee of order; the image of Charles I as 'that man of blood', responsible for bringing about the civil wars, was still a potent one. Had the Protectorate been able to offer genuine hope of a satisfactory and lasting civil settlement, the established classes might well have found it acceptable. But the truth was that Oliver Cromwell was never able to transform his military authority into a genuinely civilian one. After his death, the struggle for power within the army and among the political factions convinced all those with a vested interest in preserving stability that there really was no alternative to a return to the pre-1649 condition of things, this time with a king who would respect the limits of his power.

One of the remarkable features of the period, which continues to fascinate historians, is how productive it was in political and religious ideas. It was perhaps too productive. Mixed in with intense belief was a great deal of confusion and ambiguity of thought. It is difficult to avoid the conclusion that even in an age of religious fervour, such as the period 1640–60 was, self-interest and self-protection predominated. People seldom act out of pure principle or abstract belief. When extreme political activists or rabid religious sectaries threatened the existing social order, people were willing to see Cromwell as a guardian. But when the army demanded heavy taxation and enforced billeting of soldiers, the same people just as readily saw him as an oppressor. Behind the talk of constitutions and settlements was a deep concern to gain or retain position and privilege. This was hardly the stuff of revolution. The notion of society as a hierarchical order was far too deeply entrenched for it to be seriously threatened by the political or religious radicals.

Reference

1 John Morrill (Ed.), *Revolution and Restoration: England in the 1650s*, Collins and Brown, 1992, p. 111.

Working on Chapter 7

This chapter offers three main conclusions:

1 The importance of the Interregnum lies essentially in its negative aspects. The events of the years 1649–60 discredited a number of notions in regard to monarchy, parliament, government, army, religion, and finance.
2 There are, nevertheless, a number of positive features which should not be overlooked. Outstanding among these are foreign affairs.
3 The Interregnum, rather than being a revolutionary period, marked a retreat from revolution.

Examine these three propositions by measuring them against your own judgement, and by asking yourself how far they accord with the viewpoints of the other writers whose work you have studied on this period. If you agree with the propositions, it would be a useful exercise to note down the facts that could be used to support each of them.

Summary Diagram
The Interregnum in Perspective

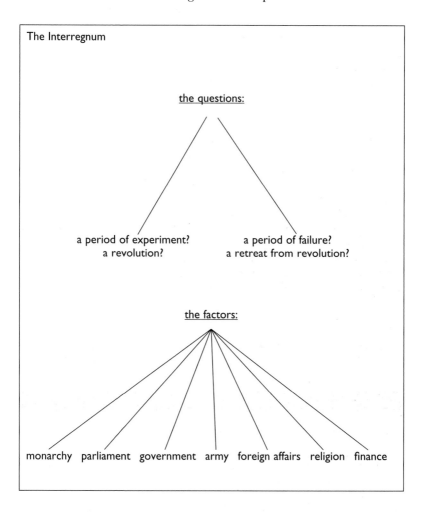

Glossary

Anti-Christ a Calvinist term applied to the damned and their behaviour

Arminianism a doctrine that rejected predestination and taught that salvation came via God's sanctifying grace as dispensed through the sacraments of the church

assessment a parliamentary tax levied monthly on land and property

Calvinism a strict form of Protestantism, deriving from the teachings of Jean Calvin (1509–64) and characterised by a belief in predestination

Covenanters Scottish Presbyterians who swore by the Solemn League and Covenant to introduce their form of worship as the state religion in England. They were the main supporters of Charles II in Scotland, 1649–51

Decimation a tax imposed during the Interregnum on known royalists

Diggers the mocking title for the 'true levellers', who called for an end of private property and set up idealistic communes in the 1650s in the belief that land belonged not to individuals but to the community

Elect the Calvinist term for those predestined for salvation

Engagers Scottish Presbyterians who took an 'Engagement' to press for the establishment of Presbyterianism as the state religion in England. Both Charles I and Charles II entered into agreements with them

Episcopacy the governing bishops within a church system

Godly as a noun referred to those predestined for salvation (alternative terms are the 'saints' or the 'elect')

Grandees the officers who belonged to the Council of the Army

Impeachment a formal vote by Parliament convicting a person of treason

Indemnity the guarantee of protection against prosecution for acts committed during the civil wars – consistently demanded by the troops throughout the Interregnum

Independents the Protestant separatist sects that refused to recognise the authority of a state church, whether Anglican or Presbyterian

Jesuits the Society of Jesus, a special order of priests set up in 1540 and dedicated to defending the Roman Catholic Church against the forces of Protestantism

Laudianism the English form of Arminianism that took its name from Archbishop Laud, who emphasised the need for conformity of worship and obedience

Levellers a radical urban movement of the 1640s that claimed that sovereignty lay not with governments but with the people

Mass the central Roman Catholic ritual, involving the act of consecration by the priest at which moment, according to believers, the sacramental bread and wine turned into the real body and blood of Christ (transubstantiation)

Mercantilism a form of trade warfare based on protectionism

Millenarianism the belief that the known world was about to end and the 1000-year reign of Christ and His saints begin

Popery an abusive Puritan term to describe Roman Catholicism

Norman Yoke the notion that the English had been a free people until 1066 when William the Conqueror and his Normans had begun to oppress them

Prayer Book the Laudian church manual, which laid down detailed regulations about the way in which public worship was to be conducted

Predestination the Calvinist belief that denied free will and held that individuals were either saved or damned from the moment of conception

Prerogative the monarch's royal power which stood outside the jurisdiction of the common law

Presbyterianism was of two distinct varieties: the dogmatic Scottish form with its belief in a strongly centralised church organised by elders, and the milder English form, sometimes known as political Presbyterianism, whose main idea was of a church without bishops

Puritanism has no precise denominational meaning; it is generally used to refer to the stricter forms of Protestant belief

Radicalism the belief that society must be not merely reformed but changed at its roots

Regicides those who signed the death warrant of Charles I

Thorough the policy of strong central government, associated with Strafford in the 1630s

Tithe a tax levied locally for the upkeep of ministers of the parish church

Triers and Ejectors a body of Commissioners, set up by Cromwell in 1653, charged with the responsibility of selecting and supervising the ministers of the church

Further Reading

There is now a wealth of excellent books on the Interregnum. The following is a very selective list of works which will be of particular interest to students.

1 General Surveys

Gerald Aylmer, *Rebellion or Revolution* (OUP, 1986), written by one of the leading authorities on Stuart history, has become a standard text. It complements an earlier and vital collection of essays which Aylmer edited: *The Interregnum: the Quest for Settlement, 1646–1660* (1972).

Toby Barnard, *The English Republic 1649–60* (Longman, 1982). This is a short but still comprehensive account, with a good selection of sources.

Samuel Gardiner, *History of the Commonwealth and Protectorate* (Longman, 1903) and **C.H. Firth**, *The Last Years of the Protectorate* (Longman, 1909). Although written a century ago, these multi-volume works are still revered by modern scholars for their combination of scholarship and flowing narrative. It would be a pity if students denied themselves the pleasure of such a good read.

Christopher Hill, *The Century of Revolution, 1603–1714* (Nelson, 1961) is just one of the very many works by the most prolific writer on the period. Hill has modified his own views since writing this, but it remains an interesting example of the determinist approach to history.

Derek Hirst, *England in Conflict 1603–60* (Hodder Headline, 1999). An important revisionist look at the period; this is well worth comparing with the preceding entry.

Ronald Hutton, *The British Republic, 1649–60* (Macmillan, 1990). Hutton is a provocative writer, concerned here with stressing that the Interregnum should be seen in a British, not just an English, context.

Mark Kishlansky, *A Monarchy Transformed: Britain 1603–1714* (Allen Lane, 1996) has illuminating chapters on the Interregnum.

John Morrill (Ed.), *Revolution and Restoration: England in the 1650s* (Collins and Brown, 1992). This is a collection of seven essays on key aspects of the period.

Ivan Roots, *The Great Rebellion 1640–60* (Batsford, 1968) continues to be regarded as one of the most interesting and reliable treatments of the period.

Conrad Russell, *The Crisis of Parliaments: English History 1509–1660* (OUP, 1971). The later chapters of this book will introduce the student to some of the key ideas of one of the leading contributors to the analysis of the English Revolution.

Alan G.R. Smith, *The Emergence of a Nation State: The Commonwealth of England 1529–1660* (Longman, 1997) contains important sections and documents relating to the Interregnum.

Austin Woolrych, *England Without a King* (Methuen, 1983) is a brief but masterful analysis by one of the acknowledged authorities on the period.

John Wroughton, *The Stuart Age 1602–1713* (Longman, 1997) is an excellent reference book with particularly helpful biographical and bibliographical sections on the Interregnum.

2 Particular Themes

The King's Trial and Execution

David Underdown, *Pride's Purge: Politics in the Puritan Revolution* (Oxford, 1971) analyses the key event that gave shape to the Interregnum.

C.V. Wedgwood, *The Trial and Execution of Charles I* (Methuen, 1961) remains the most readable and best informed study of the events surrounding Charles I's execution.

The Rump

Blair Worden, *The Rump Parliament* (CUP, 1974) is an outstanding study by an outstanding scholar.

Cromwell in Ireland

D.M.R. Esson, *The Curse of Cromwell, A History of the Ironside Conquest of Ireland, 1649–53* (Leo Cooper, 1972) is a good example of the traditional view of Cromwell as a monster in Ireland.

Jason McElligott, *Cromwell, Our Chief of Enemies* (Dundalgan Press, 1994) began the process among Irish historians of revising the traditional view.

Tom Reilly, *Cromwell, An Honourable Enemy* (Phoenix Press, 1999) is the most thorough of the modern revisionist studies providing a sympathetic picture of Cromwell.

The Nominated Assembly

Austin Woolrych, *Commonwealth to Protectorate* (OUP, 1983) provides a scholarly analysis of the 'Barebones' experiment and the creation of the Protectorate.

The Radical movements of the Interregnum:

Howard Shaw, *The Levellers* (Longman, 1968) describes and analyses the movement in a form that is especially helpful for students.

Christopher Hill, *The World Turned Upside Down* (Penguin, 1975) remains an important analysis of the fringe religious and political groups of the period. Hill's book is worth comparing with the work of the following major authority:

Gerald Aylmer, *The Levellers in the English Revolution* (OUP, 1985)

Frances Dow, *Radicalism in the English Revolution 1640–1660* (Blackwell, 1985) traces the story across the whole revolutionary period.

Robert Acheson, *Radical Puritans in England 1550–1660* (Longman, 1990) has an informative section on radical developments during the Interregnum.

The Major-Generals

Christopher Durston, *Cromwell's major-generals: Godly Government During the English Revolution*. (Manchester UP, 2001) is an informed and fascinating examination of Cromwell's remarkable experiment in military government.

The Parliaments of the Protectorate

Hugh Trevor Roper, *Religion, Reformation and Social Change* (OUP, 1967) contains a chapter 'Oliver Cromwell and his Parliaments', which remains a must for anyone seriously intending to study the theme.

The Royalists During the Interregnum

P.H. Hardacre, *The Royalists during the Puritan Revolution* (The Hague, 1956) remains the most authoritative study of how the royalists fared in this period.

David Underdown, *Royalist Conspiracy in England* (OUP, 1960) details the attempts of the royalists to challenge the Protectorate.

Ronald Hutton, *Charles II* (Oxford, 1989) is a fascinating account of Charles II in exile during the Interregnum.

Austin Woolrych, *Penruddock's Rising, 1655* (Historical Association, 1955) is a short and very readable account.

The Restoration

Ronald Hutton, *The Restoration: A Political and Religious History of England and Wales, 1658–1667* (OUP, 1985). The early chapters of this important book cover the period from the death of Oliver Cromwell in 1658 to the return of Charles II in 1660.

3 Biographies

There will doubtless never be complete agreement about the character and achievements of Oliver Cromwell, the dominant figure of the Interregnum. Of the many modern studies the following are recommended:

Blair Worden, *Roundhead Reputations: The English Civil Wars and the Passions of Posterity* (Allen Lane, 2001) is a particularly interesting and informative analysis of the different ways in which different ages have seen Cromwell. The same theme is covered at shorter length in Worden's 'The English Reputations of Oliver Cromwell 1660–1900' in *Historical controversies and historians,* edited by William Lamont, (UCL Press, 1998).

R.C. Richardson (Ed.), *Images of Oliver Cromwell* (Manchester UP, 1993) contains a series of articles tracing the changing interpretations of Cromwell and his historical importance.

C.H. Firth, *Oliver Cromwell and the Rule of the Puritans in England* (OUP, 1900). Although over a century old, this remains one of the most enlightening studies of the Protector as a person.

Barry Coward, *Oliver Cromwell* (Longman, 1991). This is a balanced, and perhaps the most accessible, modern biography of Cromwell. This should be compared with:

Christopher Hill, *God's Englishman: Oliver Cromwell and the English Revolution* (1970) provides an interpretation of Cromwell as religious zealot and bourgeois revolutionary.

Ivan Roots (Ed.) *Cromwell, a Profile* (Macmillan, 1973) is an important collection of essays by major authorities on various aspects of Cromwell's career.

Antonia Fraser, *Cromwell: Our Chief of Men* (Weidenfeld and Nicholson, 1973) is a wide-ranging and lively account of his life.

John Morrill (Ed.) *Oliver Cromwell and the English Revolution* (Longman, 1990) gathers together a number of important reappraisals of Cromwell.

Peter Gaunt, *Oliver Cromwell* (Blackwell, 1996) is a very accessible Historical Association pamphlet.

4 Sources

John Kenyon, *The Stuart Constitution* (CUP, second edition, 1986). This book has established itself as an essential source-study of the period. One of its great strengths is the quality of its linking commentaries.

5 Articles

Students who have access to historical journals will find that the following offer a very useful short cut to some of the most important studies of the period.

Peter Gaunt, 'The Single Person's confidants and dependents? Oliver Cromwell and his Protectoral councillors', *Historical Journal*, 32 (1989).

Derek Hirst, 'Concord and discord in Richard Cromwell's House of Commons', *English Historical Review*, 103 (1988).

Austin Woolrych, 'The Cromwellian Protectorate: a military dictatorship?', *History*, 75 (1990).

Austin Woolrych, 'The Good Old Cause and the fall of the Protectorate', *Historical Journal*, 13 (1957).

Blair Worden, 'Providence and politics in Cromwellian England', *Past and Present*, 109 (1985).

Index